Luv, Bonnie

A MEMOIR

Written by Bonnie Salkow

Artwork by Knucci

ISBN: 978-0-578-37679-0
Independently published

DISCLAIMER
This is a work of creative nonfiction and reflects the author's recollection of events. Names and identifying details have been changed to protect the privacy of the people involved.

This book is not intended to be used as a substitute for the advice of a relevant qualified expert.

Dedication

To Miguel Angel Falcon,

You've inspired me through the magic in your heart, your music, and Mitana. Your brilliant and creative mind, your talent, words, and your precious soul. I will forever cherish and be grateful for your friendship. Thank you for helping make my childhood dreams of becoming a performer and a star come true. Thank you for encouraging me to shine and to use my wings to fly, without which, I don't believe this book would have been written.

With love always, Bonnie

Contents

Introduction

According to my mother, she reached for a Saltine cracker on the morning of August 14, 1959, and went into labor. No coincidence I was grabbing for food even before I even came into the world!

I was their first, and only, child. We lived in Mt. Vernon, New York until I was five years old, and then we moved to White Plains, a suburb about 20 miles outside of New York City.

I've always loved dogs and have had many throughout the course of my life—my dogs were always my children, and I never wanted kids of my own.

My favorite thing in the world was to go into the city and see Broadway shows, especially musicals—that passion has stayed with me my whole life! I've always loved to dance, exercise, and go on long walks.

Competitive sports were not my thing and flying balls have always scared me. I have a HUGE fear of bugs—be it a sweet ladybug or a giant palmetto bug (an enormous flying cockroach).

I was a shy child, filled with trepidation, yet always craved the spotlight. I remember being only four years old when I was called up onto the stage with Abbe Lane, a sultry singer/performer in the early

1960s. Basking in the spotlight felt like pure magic to me and it's enticed me ever since. NOTHING, absolutely nothing, mattered more to me than becoming a star.

Although I was always smiling on the outside, I was disillusioned and carried the burden of shame for most of my life. Misery engulfed me and I couldn't seem to shake it. I never felt like I fit in and it only got worse as I got older. Mood swings and depression have haunted me from as far back as I can remember. Since I could never casually drink or take drugs, addiction swallowed me whole from the age of 20.

Despite all that darkness, I've never lost the ability to see the beauty around me in animals, nature, and creativity.

I love writing and have always been enchanted by the world of spirit, going to psychics and mediums from an early age. Their words resonated with me when they told me I'd write a book one day. However, as I rarely followed through with anything, I never imagined it would become a reality.

The year 2021 was challenging for all of us with the Covid pandemic. Despite being so very grateful to be sober since 2011, mental health issues have continued to plague me and I've been hospitalized five times in sobriety because of them. The last time I got out in April of 2021, I started writing little snippets of stories, which in time became the foundation for this book.

The writing has been cathartic, although I had no

idea how much work was involved in writing a book. There was so much to learn, and I loved the challenge of it, yet reliving those muddy waters was often tortuous because I'm not that person anymore.

In those moments, I remembered my purpose (a thing I never had until I got sober), which is helping others. The more honest I am about my experiences, the better chance I have of helping someone.

Whoever is reading this, I hope you can get something out of it. If you're going through something, perhaps my story will give you the encouragement that you can get through it, too. We are never alone. If not, I just hope that you enjoy reading it!

Luv,

Bonnie

LUV, BONNIE

LUV, BONNIE

Once Upon a Time

I'd almost made it out of the house when I heard my mother's shrill voice summoning me up to her bedroom. Irritated, she scanned me from head to toe, and burst into a tirade about my appearance, demanding that I put on something warmer. "It's not summer yet. You're going to freeze your ass off. Why do you have to keep wearing these old things when all I do is buy you new clothes? Pull back your hair. You look like a wild Indian." Why couldn't she just let me be? I changed my clothes and left for school, exasperated.

It all looked so perfect from the outside. That big corner house on a hill in White Plains, New York. Number 2 Old Farm Circle. It was a quiet neighborhood, newly developed, comprised of about 20 lavish homes filled with young parents, their small children, and pets. A suburban utopia.

Yet, there were undoubtedly scandals abounding behind closed doors. After all, I couldn't have been the only one burdened with secrets, living in the grips of isolation and despair. I don't know their stories, but I know mine all too well. A goddess of blazing destruction, haunted by addiction, driven by a million forms of fear. Blessed by a transformation beyond recognition into a world of exquisite freedom.

We moved there when I was five from our apartment in Mount Vernon. That's where I met my mother's best friend, 'Aunt Nina' and her two daughters, Ginger and Chloe. They were all at the hospital when I was born. I felt loved and safe when I was with them. Ginger and Chloe babysat for me and Aunt Nina, who at 96 years old still calls me JuJu Drops, taught my mother how to cook the most delicious Italian food ever.

I had a privileged childhood, but that didn't guarantee happiness. It was traumatic and lonely as well. Given more than my share of material things, I still felt empty and unloved inside. I'm not blaming anyone, it's just the way it was. I wondered, *Where's all the laughter and the music? Why is the mood so somber here?* I didn't feel like I belonged there.

Of course, I had my share of joyful moments, too. Playing outside, imagining what those fluffy white clouds floating across the sky really were. Parades of unicorns, hearts, pigs, and teddy bears entertained me. I created a separate world far away from the one I was living in as I inhaled the freshly mowed grass and daydreamed of happier places. Hot summer days were spent blowing bubbles and running through sprinklers.

I loved to color, do arts and crafts, and to sing and dance when no one was around. That feeling of impending doom was never far away. Longing for happiness, I looked up and kept wishing upon the stars.

I resented never knowing what kind of mood my mother would be in. Life for me meant tip-toeing around on eggshells wherever I went. She had moments of serenity, but mostly, she was a raging lunatic, exploding at the drop of a hat. There was a constant barrage of screaming, cursing, throwing things, smacking me across the face, and calling me hurtful names. If I spilled a glass of water, she'd become outraged. Her scathing words always made me tremble. "Your father is an EMOTIONAL CRIPPLE," she'd scream, just because he was watching a football game and not paying enough attention to her. She unleashed all of her anger and frustrations, and I was the usual target.

Negativity was my mother's middle name. No matter how sunny a day it was, as soon as she stepped out of the house she'd squint her eyes and say, "I should bring an umbrella. It looks like it's going to rain." To this day, I refuse to own or use an umbrella.

I was desperate to escape the house that I felt so confined to. One day, around the age of nine, I sat myself down on the cold kitchen floor with a razor-sharp knife. I was curious to see just how far I could go without piercing the delicate skin of my wrist. That little voice inside my head wondered, *What would happen if you did this?* It would have made a big mess, of course. No one wanted that. I got up, put the knife back in the drawer. I opened the freezer, blindly reached for a glazed cinnamon bun, stuffed it down my throat, and sauntered away.

Home

I loved my maternal grandparents, especially my grandmother. Without a doubt, I am certain that she is my Guardian Angel. My mother had always been terrified of her and my father never liked her. From what I understand, it's because she never felt that he was a suitable match for my mother. As much as I've always adored him, my father could be quite dismissive if he didn't like you. He called my grandmother an old witch when she was on her deathbed, going nose to nose with her, getting right up in her face. It was from that very bed, while transitioning to the other side after a 9-hour brain surgery, where she told me I was her favorite and most beautiful grandchild of them all. I felt nothing but cherished and loved around her.

I loved talking to my grandparents on the phone (In those days, there were multiple telephones scattered about the house so anyone could pick up the line and listen in while you were talking). Grandma Rozzie always loved to hear me singing, and I loved singing to them both on the phone. I was in all my glory when she praised me. "Bonnie has such a wonderful voice. Isn't that right, Willie," she'd ask my grandfather, who agreed with anything she said.

And then the other shoe would drop. Right in the middle of a song, I'd hear a click from the upstairs phone receiver as my mother picked it up and ordered me to hang up the phone. "They didn't call just to hear you sing all night. Enough already." My grandmother would always disagree with her, "Of course we did, Grace. Keep singing, Bonnie." It was music to my ears.

I spent lots of happy weekends at my grandparents' apartment in Brooklyn. They'd bring me to Coney Island, where we played games in the amusement arcades. Other times, we'd go to Jones Beach to watch dazzling shows in the outdoor amphitheater. We spent endless hours winning stuffed animals and toys, building sandcastles and collecting shells.

They let me eat all the frozen custard, french fries and cotton candy I wanted. I knew there'd be hell to pay when my mother saw my new white rabbit jacket covered in sticky pink blotches. My grandparents kept a comfy blanket on the backseat of their Cadillac for me. Wrapped up, I'd drift off to sleep after our carefree days at the beach, feeling safe and loved.

I wanted to play the piano, so my parents bought me a brand new baby grand piano. I lost interest after two years. Maybe I would have enjoyed it more had I not been pressured to practice so much.

When I wanted to be a ballerina, they signed me up for ballet lessons. My desire for a brother or sister to keep me company, my parents informed me, would never happen. Instead, when I was seven, they surprised me with a Yorkshire Terrier, the dog I'd been begging them for. Music became my new best friend.

My father grew up in a very poor family, moving whenever they couldn't pay the rent. My grandfather was an alcoholic, so my father dropped out of high school and got a job when he was 13 to help support his family who was just scraping by. I don't remember my grandfather because he passed away when I was a toddler. Though not highly educated, my father was extremely savvy and street smart. His mother, my Grandma Josephina, was sweet and soft-spoken and never spoke an unkind word about anyone. His sister, whom I've always adored, was beautiful and confident.

Although I had no respect for my mother, I'd always had the utmost respect for my father. Harry was the King. He carried the weight of the world on his shoulders and never once complained. When he was 18, he got drafted and was sent off to serve our country in World War Two. I used to love his real life war stories. I listened in awe as I pictured him storming through Normandy, enduring barbaric conditions. He marched for days on end with blisters and blood-soaked boots as he and his fellow soldiers deliriously carried on, doing whatever they had to do to survive.

I listened intently to how he'd earned all his medals and badges. With empathetic ears, I heard how he and his troop huddled in the trenches while under fire and how he endured his closest friend lying next to him, going through shell shock and being killed. I was astonished by the tale of how a medic, cigarette dangling from his mouth and ashes dropping into my father's open wound, saved my father's leg from getting amputated. I was shocked to learn my father had a swastika patch. "How do you think I got it? I ripped it off his uniform. It was a war. It was him or me," he said in his shaking voice. We never spoke about it again. I couldn't wrap my mind around it all.

My father was awarded three Purple Hearts. He survived, but endless nightmares chased him long afterwards. I was always so proud of him. Proud of all of his medals and badges. In awe of his courage and bravery. For the hero that he was and always will be.

So I understand why my depression was unfathomable to him. "JUST GET UP! What do you mean DEPRESSED?" My father never believed in psychiatrists and treatment centers and all that self-help stuff that I sought for so many years. Hard-working and ambitious, he spent most of his life working. He worked and worked. And worked some more. The last thing he ever wanted was for me or my mother to worry about money or suffer the hardships he had as a child. What a kind, simple, and humble man he was. One who couldn't have cared less what others' opinions of him were.

His way of showing love was providing for my mother and me, although I never understood why he stayed with my mother because no matter what he did, it was never good enough for her. It was only later in my life when I learned that he truly loved her.

You never knew if my father felt good or bad. He left for work before 8:00 am every Monday through Friday and the earliest he came home was around 5:30 pm. Except on very rare occasions, like a holiday or a debilitating cold.

As I got older, he'd occasionally take a Wednesday afternoon off to play golf or cards with his friends at the club. When he came home from work, even after a grueling hour-long commute, he often went straight down to the basement to work some more until he was ready to eat dinner, which my mother always had waiting for him.

The sound of the garage door opening when he arrived was my salvation. It meant a temporary reprieve from my mother's tantrums. No doubt that my insurmountable need for approval was my first addiction.

The day I got my first pair of Mary Janes, I was six years old and bursting with excitement. I ran to greet him at the garage door with my feet sparkling in patent leather and little heels clicking. All I longed for was for him to tell me how pretty I looked in my new shoes. "Look, look, LOOK! DO YOU LIKE THEM?!!"

Unless he came home early enough, I had to eat dinner with the live-in housekeepers we had. I loved them because they were always nice to me and they would never even think of criticizing me. I watched *I Love Lucy* on the TV that sat on the kitchen table and my mother often sat with us.

She had no boundaries, and I especially hated that she was constantly picking food off of my plate. When she let me eat with my father, he would read the newspaper or watch TV during dinner. So I either stared at the back of the TV (which sat in the middle of the table) or the back of the newspaper. It was rare that the three of us would just sit and talk.

Waving Through a Window

Cosmopolitan, Vogue, Harper's Bazaar, and *Elle* were just a few of my favorite magazines. I spent hours poring over their glossy pages, ripping out images of all the luxurious things that I wanted. Our house was only a five-minute drive away from Neiman Marcus, Saks Fifth Avenue, and Bloomingdales. There were some other stores but screw them. I was only interested in the best.

My mother handed over all of her credit cards when I was old enough to drive myself and go shopping after high school. I'd buy whatever I wanted and upon my return, she'd instruct me to run up to my room and hide all the packages so my father wouldn't see them. Like the good little girl I was, I did as I was told.

She was a good mother. I understand now that she was sick, and she was doing the best she could. She loved me, even if her presence triggered a burning rage and disgust inside of me. I couldn't stand being near her because her watchful eyes never seemed to let up. As a result, I was never comfortable in my own skin. I knew I'd never have children because I was terrified I would damage them like I felt she was damaging me. I couldn't bear the thought of anyone feeling the same shame and torment I'd always felt.

I can still recall the unbearable feeling of my mother

sniffing me EVERYWHERE when I was only an infant lying on the changing table.

At five, I innocently picked a flower for my mother from our neighbor's garden. When I handed it to her, she got angry and told me I needed to go back and apologize for stealing it. She picked me up to carry me to their house and, as my hand brushed against her chest, she let out a bloodcurdling scream. "NEVER TOUCH ANOTHER WOMAN LIKE THAT AGAIN!" I was horrified.

Whenever we had a school vacation, I traveled with my parents to lots of lush tropical places. We went to Puerto Rico, Florida, The Bahamas, Aruba, Curacao, Mexico, and The Virgin Islands. True, I was blessed to go on these trips, but I loathed how my mother slept in my bed because my father snored. SO WHAT? It wasn't like she couldn't hear him snoring from the next bed.

We had a housekeeper, so why did my mother feel it necessary to come into my room and collect my dirty laundry, inspect and smell my panties, and interrogate me? "Are you showering every day?" OF COURSE I was showering every day. It was humiliating.

There were two bathrooms upstairs and four people living in the house. My mother felt the need to use the bathroom I shared with the housekeeper, even though she had a master bathroom in her room. What was wrong with that one? She would leave dirty tissues and makeup scattered all over the vanity. With two enormous closets in her room, why did she need to stuff her clothes into my closet? She left her mark everywhere, edging closer and closer to me. It was infuriating.

She had this constant need to command me to stand up straight. She knocked me down at every turn, then looked over her shoulder and said to my father, "Harry, isn't she wonderful?"

At 13 years old, I came home from school one day and asked her what French kissing was. She pulled me into the bathroom and stuck her tongue in my mouth. It was traumatizing.

I despised how she waltzed around their stark, gloomy bedroom with me in the room. Sagging breasts flopping around, she'd parade around in nothing but her panties climbing on top of my father as he sat in his recliner chair and turned bright red. It was disgusting. I didn't need to see that.

When she was in there alone, why didn't she close her legs when I knocked on the door? I was enraged and repulsed every time I had to walk in to see her lying on the bed with her legs spread open and her hands between her legs.

That entire house was dark and morbid. All the windows and blinds had to stay closed, and I'd get in trouble if I opened them. I would stare out my bedroom window and wonder as my tears mixed with rage, *Does anyone see me out there?* I felt like a caged animal.

Why did she get into my bed, reeking of stale cigarettes, when I was six years old and touch me inappropriately?

After that, who WOULDN'T have slept with a chair in front of their bedroom door at night? With a pocketbook wedged up against the chair. How else would I know if the door had been opened while I was asleep? There wasn't a day in my life when I felt safe around her. Mothers hugging their daughters and them feeling safe? Was that a thing? Her touch made my skin crawl.

Why did she always have to comment on the way my body looked? "Your legs are so beautiful. Your bras don't fit properly. Stop picking your cuticles," she'd say. Leering at me in dressing rooms when we went clothes shopping, appraising my body and giving unsolicited opinions of how anything that showed off my body was too tight.

Why, when I came home from college on a holiday break, did she feel the need to pry into my personal life with my boyfriend? "Are you and Anthony having sex? Does he go down on you?" The LAST thing I wanted to hear was how much she loved oral sex and how my father wouldn't give it to her because he thought it was dirty. Was she fucking kidding me? It made me cringe and the repercussions of that conversation were catastrophic. How does one get THAT out of your head?

A Spoonful of Sugar

Then there's the whole eating thing. A whole other level of crazy. Our pantry door made a faint squeak whenever it opened, so I was as quiet as a mouse whenever I opened it. Even from upstairs, she had the uncanny ability to hear that little squeak. She could even hear the refrigerator door open. It was amazing. She would come flying down the staircase like a bat with sonar straight into the kitchen. Like the chief of the food police, she'd say, "CRACKERS ARE FATTENING IF YOU EAT ENOUGH OF THEM."

That woman hopped on the scale from five to ten times a day. "I REALLY SHOULDN'T EAT THIS." She'd berate herself every time she ate anything with over twenty calories. "I have to lose these five pounds. Look at my stomach." *No thanks, YOU look at your stomach,* I thought. She only wore a size 8, not fat by ANY standards. Suddenly, I began believing that if I were to even gain an ounce, I'd be fat. My thinking was becoming just as twisted as hers.

One evening, my father finished eating dinner and my mother trailed off behind him. I'm left sitting alone at the kitchen table with a mouthful of food. Swallowing what's left in my mouth in disbelief as I hold back my tears, I polish off everything on my plate and step over to the stove. As I shovel down spoonfuls of rice, I'm careful to leave just enough in the pot so that no one will see how much I've eaten. I then walk over to the freezer where I take out a gallon size container of coffee ice cream. Silently pulling off the top, I place it ever so gently down on the formica countertop. I can feel my heart slowing down with each spoonful of luscious cold ice cream that slides down my throat. The faster I eat, the calmer I become.

Taken from my diary...

1968 (9 years old)

Dear Diary,
I had a date with Kara. We made cookies. I couldn't eat any because of my diet. I don't mind because it will help me lose weight by not eating any. And, you know what? I didn't cheat! I'm so glad I lost 3 pounds altogether!

Dear Diary,
I went off my diet. I had salad and a corned beef sandwich for dinner. Mustard too.

1969 (10 years old)

Dear Diary,
Today, I went to Sunday School. We made noodle pudding, and I didn't taste it because of my diet. For dinner, I went off my diet a little. We had Chinese food and then Baskin and Robbins ice cream. It was delicious.

1970 (11 years old)

Dear Diary,
Started Water Diet. Didn't drink enough water.

Dear Diary,
I'm still on my diet. Hamburger for dinner. It was yucky.

Dear Diary,
I had veal cutlet parmigiana on Italian bread. I went off my diet.

1971 (12 years old)

Dear Diary,
Charlotte told me about The Atkins Diet.

Dear Diary,
Today I went off my diet. I chewed two pieces of gum.

1972 (13 years old)

Dear Diary,
Broke my diet and was mad. I want a good figure so badly!!

Dear Diary,
Charlotte and I started The Ice Cream Diet.

1973 (14 years old)

Dear Diary,
Stuck to my diet. Yay! So mad I ever went off!

Dear Diary,
Mommy took me to the corner to get donuts for
the bake sale and I got Hostess Snowballs. Had
shrimp and Dr. Pepper for dinner. It was so good!

I was only 15 when my mother decided I was looking somewhat bloated and one of her water pills would help. Water pills, more commonly known as diuretics, are used to treat several medical conditions including heart failure, high blood pressure, liver disease and some types of kidney disease. They also reduce swelling and water retention.

My mother had none of these. What she had was an obsession with her weight and one pill could have you dropping one to three pounds on the scale overnight. She always kept a supply in her medicine cabinet.

The downside is that they can cause electrolyte and mineral loss, dehydration, muscle cramps, heart irregularities and kidney damage. Especially when taken over time or in large amounts. I was only going to take one, so why not?

After popping my first water pill and getting that enormous rush of excess water depleted from my perfectly thin adolescent body, I learned something. Any time I felt the slightest bit of bloat, all I had to do was pop a pill and it would magically disappear. It was quite a rush. I began stealing them from her occasionally for a quick fix here and there. They were prescribed by her doctor and extremely potent. One pill and I was gushing out water.

The overeating that I'd dabbled with in high school (sneaking into the pantry for snacks while doing my homework) turned into full-blown bingeing my freshman year in college. I even found a doctor to write me a prescription for diuretics.

By Thanksgiving break, I'd already put on the Freshman 15 that you hear about. To avoid inevitable scrutiny, I came up with an excuse not to go home for the holiday and stayed in the dorms with a few other strays. I'm guessing very few of them were there because they'd put on a couple of pounds and were afraid of what their mothers would have to say about it. She meant well. She really did.

The summer after my sophomore year, my mother marched me straight to a diet doctor who gave me all kinds of colorful pills. I wouldn't be OK until I looked the way she wanted me to look. Any fat on my body, real or imagined, was unacceptable to her. Unfortunately, by this point, it had become unacceptable to me as well.

Bulimia is binge eating and purging through vomiting, exercise, laxatives, or diuretics. Some or all of the above. Considered a mental illness, it affects millions of people, male and female. Eating disorders are deadly. It's currently estimated that over 10,000 people die and commit suicide per year because of them. That's one person every 52 minutes.

Many believe that bulimics must vomit. Not true. I never did, somehow making me believe for years that I was different. I never vomited. SO WHAT? I was still a RAGING bulimic. Bulimarexic, actually. Every waking thought was about body image and the quest to be thin. Nothing and no one mattered more.

Thus began a lifetime of insanity in the hamster wheel of me trying to control my weight, no matter how high the cost. No matter how good I looked, I never thought I looked good enough. I wasn't thin enough or pretty enough or sexy enough. The scale ruled my life. My only goal in life was getting to 128 pounds. Once I got there, that wasn't good enough, so I had to get to 125 pounds. Then to 123 pounds.

After that, why not break the teens and hit 118 pounds? How was I going to stay at that weight? Not to mention that my ass wasn't tight enough and my boobs weren't perky enough. I had become my mother and I hated myself.

Finally, the day came when I woke up and realized that I finally WAS thin enough. I had actually stayed thin enough for quite some time. Only when I stared back at my blank reflection in the mirror, I wondered when all those lines had gotten on my face. What the hell had happened?

LUV, BONNIE

Brooklyn

The ultimate escape and greatest time was always waiting for me in Brooklyn with Aunt Carol, Grandma Josephina, and my cousins. Grandma Josephina was the kindest soul you'd ever want to meet. With her frail arthritic hands, she used to knit beautiful sweaters, scarves and hats for us. She made sure I was the first of my friends to own one of the trendy crochet hats made famous by Ali MacGraw in *Love Story*. Mine was even more special because she made it for me.

Grandma Josephina lived in the basement of the 2 story family home in Brooklyn where Carol, my father's sister, and Ira, her husband, lived with my cousins Sue and Sheree. My cousins and I are all two years apart, with me right in the middle. Being there with them was where I felt most at home. And the bond that we all shared was that we all worshipped my father.

Aunt Carol was PERFECT in my eyes. She was a demigoddess who could do no wrong. Up before us all with her Twiggy lashes and makeup on, she'd pop over to her closet and throw on something phenomenal to start the day. She'd encourage me to wear whatever I wanted from her wardrobe—what a treat THAT was! She always had impeccably manicured nails and blonde hair teased as high as the sky. Her nose had been perfectly sculpted, and I was obsessed as far back as I can remember with getting a nose job like hers.

My mother insisted she had an awful nose job, which wasn't surprising. She never had a pleasant word to say about Carol. Unlike my mother, Aunt Carol would never have stayed in a robe all morning or embarrassed my cousins by driving them to school with a coat over her nightgown.

Uncle Ira always left at the crack of dawn to take out his fishing boat charters in Sheepshead Bay or to check in on his car dealerships. He worked hard but always dropped off a bag of delicious hot fresh bagels for us first that filled the house with the most heavenly scent. There's nothing like a hot Brooklyn bagel.

My snobby mother grew up in Sheepshead Bay overlooking those same fishing boats, so it was ironic how she turned up her nose whenever Uncle Ira mentioned them. She never turned down a chance to scoff at him for doing whatever he could do to make an honest living. Her disdain for him and others on my dad's side of the family was clear. That fueled my anger for her even more.

Aunt Carol loved taking me and my cousins shopping in all the trendiest stores where we found the wildest clothes and shoes. The higher the heels and platforms, the better. It was the 70s after all.

She even brought us to some of the hottest showrooms of 70s designers in the city, so we could have all the newest styles before they hit the stores. I was always swept up in the illusion that all that outside stuff would make me OK and somehow erase the gut-wrenching sadness I was feeling inside.

At home or in the car, it was nothing but good times as we sang and danced along to all the hit songs. Their favorite music became my favorite music. Those were the days of Barry White, Diana and Marvin, Bette Midler and Rod Stewart. There wasn't a lyric we hadn't memorized. I'll cherish those memories and songs forever.

In Brooklyn, even cleaning the house was a fun and playful game as my cousins and I frolicked around the living room dusting and climbing on ladders to see just how sparkly we could make the mirrors and windows. MY mother wouldn't allow me to clean at home. "Let the housekeeper do it!" I even took on the classic Brooklyn accent so I could sound more like my aunt and cousins.

An excerpt from my diary....

1973 (14 years old)

Dear Diary,
Today, Sheree, Grandma, Carol and Ira came here. Sue didn't come because she had to go to someone's Sweet 16 Party. Grandma bought me two Match II tops. They're both really nice. One's long sleeve and the other is a short sleeve. I wanted to see The Poseidon Adventure when they left, but we didn't (me, Mommy, Daddy). I knew they were going to leave early (Sheree, grandma, Carol and Ira), and they did.

Their house in Brooklyn was a haven for me my whole life. Even many years later, when my friend Joelle and I left college in the middle of the night to get away, that's where we went. Getting away from yourself never does work, though.

We were higher than a pair of kites and if not for a sharp turn on a dark interstate highway somewhere in Maryland, we would have collided head-on with a gigantic 18-wheeler in her brand new Firebird, the IT car of the early 80s.

Gasping for air, we pulled over to the side of the road. I'm not sure what combination of drugs we had taken, but I remember waking up and opening my eyes in my cousin's bed as my grandmother sat in a chair next to the bed, gazing down at me with a broken heart. I'd been sleeping on and off for two days. My family never called the hospital, but, to my chagrin, they called my father, who wasn't the least bit thrilled.

No one on that side of the family believed in going away to college. Sue commuted into the city after high school to attend New York University's Dentistry Program and, after she graduated, became an assistant for a dentist in Sheepshead Bay until the day he retired. His office was only a few miles from the house, where she lived until she got married.

After graduating high school, Sheree started out as a teller at Citibank and, now, 40 years later, is a Vice President Branch Manager. They thought that my drug and alcohol addiction was mostly because of my fancy college and fancy friends. By the time I went off to college, I was already a train wreck just waiting to happen. My demise was inevitable. It wasn't the college or the friends that were the problem. It was me.

Cats

Holidays were never a big deal while I was growing up. As much as I was dying to celebrate Christmas and decorate a tree with lots of sparkly tinsel and lights, my mother wouldn't hear of it. She said Jews didn't celebrate Christmas.

We got together with family on some of the Jewish holidays, but we weren't religious. The dusty menorah came out of hiding for Chanukah once in a while, and I had the fun job of lighting the candles.

My parents joined a temple and sent me to Sunday School, which I hated. I had no interest in learning about Judaism and felt totally out of place with the other kids, who seemed to embrace their Jewish roots. For two years, they dragged me to services on the high holidays, until my parents cut all ties with the temple. And that was that.

For Passover, my maternal grandparents usually came to our house with my mother's brother, wife and their three kids. They came charging into the house like a pack of hungry wolves, devouring every bite of food that was laid out as if they hadn't eaten in weeks.

Uncle Dick was an MD who specialized in pathology. As if that wasn't creepy enough, he had a gruesome sense of humor and sported a full grizzly beard and long greasy hair. I was terrified of him.

Sawyer, who was my age and the oldest of the three, was the golden child. He could do no wrong in Uncle Dick's black, beady eyes. River, the middle child, was usually glued to the side of his younger sister Peyton, and the two of them were pretty much lost in their own secret world blending into the woodwork. Aunt Anneli was European (which my mother found amusing) and never had much to say to anyone.

If they didn't visit us, we'd have to go to their house in Upstate New York. I would rather have chewed glass than go there. It was a 2-hour drive each way and both my parents were heavy smokers which was torture. My mother smoked cigarettes the whole time while my father puffed away on his cigars. I had to beg them to open the windows and if I was lucky, they would crack one of them open. I sat alone in the back seat and felt like I was trapped in hell.

When we finally arrived at the house, we were greeted by Cujo, their formidable German Shepherd who was always running amok on the property, chasing wild animals. The house was hidden so deep in the woods that I wouldn't have been surprised had Hansel and Gretel come to greet us. What a funhouse it was.

There were also seven cats pussyfooting around the place, which always sent my mother, who was terrified of cats, over the edge. "Oh my God! HOW MANY OF THESE THINGS ARE THERE? Get this fucking cat away from me!" she'd scream throughout the day. Those cats had their paws everywhere, and in everything, including the strange concoctions Aunt Anneli served. Filling up on her mouthwatering European-style salads before the meal was the perfect excuse to skip the wildlife disguised as the main course.

Uncle Dick turned out to be a real dick. He stopped talking to my mother when my grandfather passed away. It became a whole money thing. I heard River committed suicide and Peyton passed away from cancer after fulfilling her lifelong dream of becoming a horticulturist. Sawyer became a ski instructor when, after two years, he dropped out of medical school. From golden child to snowman.

I contacted Frosty via email when my mother became extremely ill, hoping he could persuade my uncle to reach out to her, but he never did. I wrote them all off a very long time ago, with no love lost there. I never spoke to any of them after I turned 21.

Yom Kippur, the holiest day of the Jewish year, is the holiday where Jews are supposed to atone for their sins, asking for forgiveness through fasting and prayer to be a better person the next year. Synagogue. Reflection. Quiet stuff like that. We usually spent Yom Kippur with my father's side of the family, who were even less Jewish than we were. The day was usually spent at the racetrack, followed by Chinese food for dinner. Those were truly the best of times.

Despite not being religious, my parents always observed the one tradition of lighting a Yahrzeit Memorial Candle on the eve of Yom Kippur for their parents. The Hebrew (which I don't speak) meaning of Yahrzeit is 'soul candle', lit in memory of those who've passed, in Judaism.

I have always done the same ever since my parents passed. These candles are made to burn for 24 hours. The first time I lit one for my father, it remained flickering for close to 48 hours, which is almost unheard of. I knew it was a sign from him that he was still with me. I am always comforted by the fact that I am never alone. My Angels are always with me.

Friendship

Throughout my childhood, I shied away from cliques. I thought if people really got to know me, they wouldn't want me as their friend. I was a real goody-two-shoes, all smiles on the outside and a straight-A student.

Never feeling like I fit in, I usually stayed close to two or three friends at a time and there were three types of friends I typically chose. Those that weren't that popular, so I could hide behind them, remain invisible, and disappear from the crowd or those that were already popular, so I'd feel popular just by hanging around them. Then there were those who fed my insecurities, allowing me to continue to feel bad about myself.

Take Laura, for example. Not bad-looking, but she definitely wasn't winning any beauty contests. I wonder what was going on in her house that compelled her to give me these degrading writing assignments whenever she got mad at me. She'd stare me down with those icy blue eyes of hers, barking orders at me. "You need to write YOU ARE MY MASTER AND I AM YOUR SLAVE 100 times and hand it in to me by tomorrow."

I'd go home, slouch down over the kitchen table, and stoically do the assignment like it was homework. I couldn't stand her, but I still did the assignments.

Melissa was as sweet as apple pie and I loved hanging out with her. My mouth waters when I think of the lunches her mom Amber used to make for us—wagon wheel shaped pasta with hot, melted butter and salt. Simple but heavenly delicious—comfort food for my aching soul. The whole Norman Rockwell family vibe of her home felt like a cozy slipper to me. A respite from the harshness of my home.

I always wanted to go to my friends' houses after school because I was happier there than at home. When Charlotte moved from Riverdale to White Plains, not only did we become best friends, but so did our mothers. We'd have after school homework/play dates, usually in the den or our bedrooms. We'd steer clear of whatever room our mothers were in across the house, so as not to get asphyxiated by the heavy smoke and gossip.

Charlotte was friends with the popular kids and left me hanging in the dust after two years of being my best friend. Her mother, Lizzie, and mine remained best friends until my mother passed while I spent years hiding in the shadow of Charlotte's uber successful career and perfect life.

My friend Lisa and her sharp-tongued mother Belinda were a team I'd never fully be a part of. Their secrets knew no bounds, and I'd never be privy to half of them. I'd known Lisa since the age of five and we were inseparable, but it wasn't until high school that we spent almost every second together. Even then, I still felt like an outsider. We either slept at my house or hers, where I'd stay in and study and she'd go out and party. She had her boyfriends, and

I had my homework, my ice cream and my resentments.

More excerpts from my diary…

1969 (10 years old)

> *Dear Diary,*
> *Laura asked me to go skating, and I got a blister. She paid no attention to me, only to Piper.*

> *Dear Diary,*
> *Autumn and I watched 'Dark Shadows' after school. She pretended to be Angelique, and I was mad because I didn't want to be Barnabas. We had fun jumping on the furniture until Mommy came home.*

1970 (11 years old)

> *Dear Diary,*
> *Today I had a date with Laura. It wasn't so much fun. I don't like Laura a lot.*

1971 (12 years old)

> *Dear Diary,*
> *I thought my longest nail broke. Laura and Venus and I filed it. Wasn't even broken. I'm so mad!! I don't think Venus likes me anymore.*

1972 (13 years old)

> *Dear Diary,*
> *In my classes, I didn't work, everyone was signing yearbooks. Nikki signed something nice in my*

yearbook (nicer than what she wrote in Charlotte's). I was so glad.

1973 (14 years old)

Today I came to school with the white painter pants I bought this weekend. Charlotte was so jealous. She makes me sick.

1974 (15 years old)

Dear Diary,
Nikki's getting friendlier with Charlotte...Shit.

Apparently, even my friends made me sick. Truth is, when you don't love yourself, it's impossible to care about anyone.

Popular

I was terrified knowing only one person on the plane ride from JFK to Denver International Airport. What if I didn't meet anyone else who liked me? I was 15 years old, traveling cross-country with my childhood friend Melissa on my first *Teen Tour*.

A *Teen Tour* is a bunch of rich, spoiled kids who travel on planes and buses with a tour guide who takes them sightseeing through the country (or countries). The following summer, I went on a *Teen Tour* to Europe where I traveled throughout seven countries in Europe. I was too young or too oblivious to appreciate Europe and all it offered, although I appreciated the beauty of Capri and the deliciousness of gelato in Italy.

Melissa and I were on *Merry Time Teen Tours American Beauty Tour*, staying in comfortable hotels all across the country. Other tours were more outdoorsy, with lots of camping and youth hostels. That wasn't for me.

In my desperation to be liked by the cool kids from The Five Towns, a pretentious suburban enclave on the South Shore of Long Island, I turned my back on Melissa and almost ignored her for the entire tour. She was one of my comfort friends and I wasn't sure if my new friends would accept her. Or, if I'm being totally honest, I was being selfish. I was too concerned about them liking me to worry about anyone else. I was also consumed with guilt because I knew how cruel I was being.

Us 'cool kids' claimed ownership of the back of the bus. I wanted what they had. The designer clothes, expensive cars, nose jobs, the feeling of belonging which none of that other stuff ever could have given me (of course I didn't know that then).

There were a few guys on the tour, but mostly girls. That was fine because I was terribly shy around boys. We'd play games like the *Alphabet Game* and 20 questions, listened to music, and sang songs on our long bus rides. I was obsessed with Elton John's *Tiny Dancer* and the lyrics became my mantra as we rolled across the country. Finn was someone I met on the tour about three weeks before he got kicked off for smoking pot in Disneyland.

About six months after the tour ended, he invited a group of us to his father's party in their Fifth Avenue loft. His father is one of the most successful music producers in the world. The party was crawling with famous Grammy award-winning musicians.

Lost in an endless sea of faces, drifting around amidst the glitz and glam of the celebrity world, I felt disconnected. Especially from Finn. Technically, we weren't even friends, as I'd only known him for a few weeks and we barely even spoke on the tour. Somehow, in my mind, we were close enough for me to let everyone I met from that day on, know that we were friends because his father was so famous. As if that was going to make me someone special.

Greyson was the cutest of all the guys on the tour. He was kind of shy but definitely cool because he was from The Five Towns and that was enough to qualify him in my book. He made these adorable flirty faces where he made this hissing sound with his tongue, teeth and lips. We nicknamed him *Planters* after Planters Peanuts. I never knew why, but I went along with it.

My 16th birthday in New Orleans was epic as we danced and laughed our way through the streets. It felt like the jazz music and all the festivities were set up just for me and my birthday celebration. It was the last stop of the tour and I finally felt a part of things. I read all of my birthday cards, opened my gifts and it was a glorious night of good, clean celebrating. No drugs. No alcohol. Just pure friendship and fun.

I will always cherish the magic and beauty of the places that we saw that summer. Hiking through the intoxicating Colorado mountains, kicking back in the quaint town of Jackson Hole, Wyoming, being hypnotized by the brilliant colors of Grand Canyon and Bryce Canyon, taken aback by the aroma of damp moss amidst the splendor of the giant trees in Yosemite National Park. I remember being irritated by the mosquitoes buzzing around the park, which disturbed me more than the thought of running into a bear.

The sunlight as it reflected off the snow-covered earth at Lake Tahoe took my breath away. We were in God's country and it was glorious. California, where I splashed through the refreshing giant waves of the Pacific Ocean and bubbled over with excitement at the thought of bumping into an actual celebrity, was my favorite. I could barely contain myself when I met Billy Curtis, one of the Munchkins from the *Wizard of Oz*. It was like lollipops were falling from the sky! I was only a few licks away from stardom!

LUV, BONNIE

3

LUV, BONNIE

All That Jazz

Oh, that euphoric feeling every time the curtain goes up when I see a live show... I get the chills! There's nothing like it! When I was a child growing up in New York, my father would buy us tickets to the most fabulous shows—always the best seats.

I would stare up at the stage with utmost intensity, right into the faces of iconic stars like Patti LuPone, Gwen Verdon, Chita Rivera, Joel Grey, and Liza Minnelli. We were up so close I could see the sweat pouring down their faces. I was entranced by it all. The sparkling costumes, the glitz, the glam, the original musical scores, the dancing, and STARS! As I sat on the edge of my seat, the exquisite lure of performing filled my head, heart, and soul. I craved to be up on that stage.

It was a gift getting to see so many Tony Award-winning shows. I saw *Grease, Pippin, Cabaret, Hair, Liza with a Z, Follies,* Bette Midler's *Clams on the Half Shell, A Chorus Line, Chicago, The Wiz, Evita, Sweeney Todd,* and dozens more!

The enormously creative Bob Fosse swept me off my feet! His signature moves were unlike any other. Jazz hands, shoulder rolls, sideways shuffling, and turned in knees and toes. With a tip of a bowler hat and the tap of a cane, I instantly skyrocketed to another dimension. I became Roxie, listening to her.

Think of those autographs I'll sign. I'm a star! The audience loves me! Oh, how I longed to be on that stage from as far back as I can remember. I wanted to be an actress, a singer, a dancer—A STAR!

It's 1974. Hairbrush in hand (my microphone), I'm losing myself in the blaring music, dancing and singing in front of my bedroom mirror. My mother's piercing voice echoes from downstairs, "BONNIE! Lower that GOD DAMNED STEREOOOOOOOO!" Jolted back into reality, my performance comes to an abrupt end. Storming off my imaginary stage, cursing my mother under my breath, I began violently shaking. My audience would have to wait.

I'm Not That Girl

I'd been dying to leave home for years. But not for college. What I wanted was to go to California and become an actress. My parents insisted I go to college if I wanted their financial support. They'd paid for everything my whole life, so I didn't have a clue what I'd do if I had to support myself.

In high school, I worked in a clothing boutique but, technically—it was just a few hours after school once or twice a week to escape having to go home. I greeted customers and picked out the clothes I wanted my mother to buy me when she picked me up at the end of the day.

I'd always done what I was told to—following my dreams was never even an option. I had no confidence, no ambition, and no money of my own. My priorities were looking good and finding a guy who was rich and good-looking to fix me—someone that would finally make me OK.

Once I'd resigned myself to going to college, my first choice was to find a school in California. Too far away, they told me. So I lowered my expectations and said I'd go to Miami. "You'll be too busy getting a tan to go to classes." Like Goldilocks choosing a bed, I conceded that American University in Washington, D.C. was my best option. Not too hot, not too cold. The weather seemed OK.

There was a slight possibility I'd fit in since AU was known as a JAP (Jewish American Princess) school, and just maybe I would find my Prince Charming. Education and career choices never really played into my decision. I had the grades. It was a wonderful school, and I could figure out what I wanted to be other than an actress once I got there.

It was the first day of school at student orientation when, lo-and-behold, I spotted Greyson from my *Teen Tour.* I couldn't have been happier to see him, as I yelled his name and batted my eyelashes across the room. He'd already been there for several weeks since he'd attended the summer program, so he'd already made quite a few friends. After judging them all, I decided I wanted to be friends with them, too. I was ready to begin my first semester of college.

Since Lisa (my high school bestie), and I went to AU together, it was only natural that we were roommates. Two of our new friends, Savannah and Alissa, who'd gone to the summer program with Greyson, were also roommates. Within a few months, we became known as *The Four Musketeers.*

We were quite popular, which was a pleasant surprise. I never had a boyfriend in high school, but I was obsessed with Cole Staffordshire, who'd never given me the time of day. Now, in college, I became obsessed with Greyson's roommate Cameron, who wasn't at all into me either.

Savannah hooked up with Brody, a sophomore. Lisa attached herself to Danny, another sophomore.

Alissa seemed to be the obsession of every guy in school, teasing each one of them. The one she chose as her boyfriend was Greyson. Yes, MY Greyson.

Alissa was prettier than me, had a better body than me, and was from a beautiful home and picture-perfect family in prestigious Oyster Bay, on Long Island. She quickly became my best friend, and I envied everything about her.

While those around me were losing their virginity, I was saving myself for a fairy tale romance. I want to make sure that he LOVES me—I told myself.

It was the beginning of my sophomore year when I took one look at Anthony and I melted like hot chocolate. He was Greyson's best friend from high school and quite an elusive character, which is most likely why I hadn't met him sooner. Greyson and their friends used to call him *Tomfoolery*. I wouldn't say that he lied, per se, but he had so many far-fetched stories up his sleeve you didn't know which was real or imaginary.

Cinema Italiano

Anthony. He was the most enchanting guy I'd ever met, with a mischievous twinkle in his eye and a smile that could put the Cheshire Cat to shame. His olive skin was as smooth and flawless as silk, a gift from his Italian mother and Irish father. He charmed the pants right off of me—literally. Anthony was my first love.

Lost in the love songs on the radio, we drove through the streets of Georgetown in his red Alfa Romeo convertible with the top down, wind blowing through our hair. All around us, fall leaves rustled against an endless blue sky. It was a day made just for us. I was soaring. This was a natural high. With no drugs or alcohol. One of those moments frozen in time that I'll never forget.

Anthony grew up in the lap of luxury. His father owned *Banana Splits*, a sweet paradise of candies and decadent desserts. Anthony bragged about his father's connection to one of the most powerful crime families in history, but despite many legal allegations against him (including being the suspected mastermind of a multi-million dollar racketeering lawsuit), nothing was ever proven. It all seemed so enticing to me - pure romance and roses. I didn't need anyone or anything else. All I wanted to do was stare into his caramel eyes and get lost in them forever.

He promised to take me to his family's dude ranch in upstate New York, so we planned a trip during our Christmas break. Bags packed, slaying it in my brand new Frye boots, I galloped around my parents' house waiting for him to pick me up. I waited. Then I waited some more. I called him again and again, but he didn't answer.

He never came to pick me up. My excitement faded. It wasn't until days later that he called with some crazy excuse I fell hook, line, and sinker for. My parents weren't buying it. They didn't want me to see him, but I didn't care.

I was caught up in my fairy tale. Girl loves boy. Boy loves girl. They live happily ever after. The reality was girl loves a boy. Boy tucks girl into bed in her dorm room and stays up all night snorting coke and having sex with other girls and boys. Boy gets kicked out of school. The girl feels lost without him. She drinks more and starts using recreational drugs. Girl then sleeps with the boy's best friend (Greyson) who is also sleeping with the girl's best friend AND roommate (Alissa). Some fairy tale.

Greyson and I were in a lot of the same classes, I imagine, because neither one of us had a clue what we wanted to major in. Spaceship Earth, one of our classes, should have been called Airheads, because that's what most of us were in that class.

Alissa came up with the brilliant idea that I sleep at Greyson's house one night. He lived off campus, and we headed off to what was the beginning of a yearlong affair. It was all fun and games when we were together, but the party always came to a halt when he dropped me back off at campus.

On weekends, Alissa was the one he was wining and dining while I stayed behind, scarfing down Oreos in our dorm room. They often insisted I join them, so I'd tag along feeling like a pathetic third wheel. Poor me, I told myself. First Anthony leaves me and now I'm not good enough to be Greyson's girlfriend. I was feeling out of place and alone, yet again.

In a World of My Own

American University, despite its reputation for high-quality education, was also quite the party school. From the moment I had my first drink, one was never enough. Quaaludes (synthetic, barbiturate-like, central nervous system depressants) were all the rage back then. About ten minutes after taking one, my fingers would go numb and eventually everything else did, too. If one was good, two were better. They were even better when I swallowed them down with alcohol. I'd black out and wake up with bruises all over my body the next morning, clueless about what had happened the night before. I loved them.

After all, Greyson had Alissa. Anthony had left me. I wasn't about to honor my morals or principles because I had none. So I became sexually promiscuous, hoping to prove to myself that I could find someone to love me and not abandon me.

I spent hours on end with Kermit, who'd been friends with both Anthony and Greyson since childhood. We'd blast music in his dorm room, alternating between The Doors and The Cars, two of Kermit's favorites.

Despite having a great sense of humor, he wasn't big on conversation, so we sat around smoking pot (which only made me more paranoid than I already was) and listening to the music. That was never a problem because Kermit was great looking and I would have been happy doing nothing but staring at him for hours at a time. Out of the blue, he'd leap high in the air, put on his sunglasses, and start pacing about. He was quite a character. It's hard to remember so much of what happened because of all the drugs I was doing.

I'm pretty sure we never slept together. We may have, but did it really even matter? How many of these guys that grew up together could I sleep with in one year, anyway?

I was spinning in a million different directions as I sought to find some sense of comfort. My drug and alcohol addictions were out of control. My food binges were getting worse, I was purging more frequently, and I was increasing the number of diuretics I was taking.

By now, I was abusing laxatives as well. Despite my friend Minnie Minkelstein's excitement over her newfound secret that chocolate chip mint ice cream tasted better coming up than it did when going down, I just couldn't bring myself to vomit. Friends who weren't bulimic didn't get that polishing off an entire box of Captain Crunch in one sitting was no big deal and I no longer felt the need to be humiliated by that kind of thinking.

So I gravitated to friends that would stay up until 2 am with me for the nightly delivery of Krispy Kreme donuts to the dorms. We'd get an entire box and devour them. We'd blow off our classes that day and head across the street to Community Market, where we'd buy tons of binge foods and race back to the dorms for synchronized shitting from all the laxatives. Gross, yes, but it was my reality.

Raging with jealousy and filled with resentments, I finally told Alissa about me and Greyson after a year of sneaking around. She stormed off, left our dorm room, and never spoke to me again. It seemed like the entire school knew about it. I went from being *Miss Popularity* to a social pariah. A light switch turned off, and I was left standing in the dark. So I just buried myself deeper in my own world.

Junior year rolled into senior year and it all became one big blur. I'd long since shed that good girl image. My grades had dropped drastically since I rarely went to classes anymore.

There were so many guys I'd slept with that I started making lists. I couldn't even remember half their names. Once I hit the 100 mark, I stopped counting. Three in one day? No big deal. That hot bunch of ZBT frat boys that came down to visit from Syracuse University one weekend? Well, who could resist? One was better looking than the next. One stole something from my dorm room. Or did I steal something from his friend's dorm room?

Although loneliness can't actually kill you, my feelings of emptiness killed my spirit. While in active addiction, there's no chance of connecting with anyone or anything other than your drug of choice. Addiction is a disease of isolation, and nothing matters more than getting that drug.

I was forced to stay the summer semester after graduation to take Statistics for the third time in order to get my degree, a BA in Psychology. I was lucky to make it out of there alive, but I was finally a college graduate. That and a token would get me on the New York Subway.

New York, New York

I needed a job. Writing was something I'd always loved doing, but I had no experience as a professional writer. I did, however, know how to type.

When *Azul & Bleu* hired me as a secretary in their Media Department, I was pretty happy. It wasn't like they hired me to star in a Broadway musical, but working for the 5th largest advertising agency in the world sounded good enough for me. I quickly worked my way into the Creative Department, where I felt my talents were better suited.

Now what I needed was an apartment in Manhattan. The prices were sky high, but I was still hoping my parents would buy me one. After all, didn't I deserve a little something after getting through four tortuous years of college? "You seem to think we have a money tree in our backyard," was their response. "Get a roommate if you want to live in the city."

Brynn, a friend of mine from American University, was living in this upscale studio apartment in Murray Hill that her father had purchased for her. I couldn't bear one more minute of living with my parents and commuting. So when Brynn suggested I move in and split the rent, I immediately accepted. My parents, most likely sick of me too, generously agreed to pay the rent.

The apartment was an L-shaped studio with Venetian blinds separating me from her bedroom. I slept on a pull-out sofa in the living room and it was perfect. Greyson and I had never stopped seeing each other despite all the other guys I'd been with, and he spent almost as much time there as I did. Brynn got along famously with him and she never seemed to mind him being there.

She worked in the garment center for her father and spent most of her spare time flitting about the city with lots of gorgeous men, doing lots of drugs, and entertaining in her bordello-like bedroom with her huge heart-shaped bed and baby blue velvet bedspread.

I adored Brynn's family. Her parents lived in a beautiful home on Long Island. Skye, her mother, was all elegance, sophistication, glamour and gorgeousness. Her classy, handsome father, Ike, was a handsome combo of the perfect husband, father, and provider. Brynn was and always has been, daddy's little girl.

There was Quinn, Brynn's bubbly and sweet younger sister. The playful family dog Nathan, a Doxie, was named after the famous hot dogs. Skye referred to her girls as Brynnie and Quinnie, which I thought was as fabulous as everything else about her.

The building I worked in was in Midtown Manhattan, and the entire building was occupied by *Azul & Bleu*. I spent my days typing and gallivanting from floor to floor, hunting down all the cute guys in the building. I took full advantage of the notorious 2-hour lunches in the world of advertising by drinking the hours away. Mexican food meant margaritas, Italian food meant wine, Japanese meant Saki. Deciding where to go for lunch was more about what we were in the mood to drink. *Happy Hour* around the city, keeping up with all the hottest spots and hooking up with good-looking guys was my focus after work.

Zachary was especially memorable and someone I'll always cherish. When he walked into a room, all eyes were on him. I'll never forget the time he twirled me around in my silver fox coat, then picked me up and carried me down the staircase in the middle of Grand Central Station as everyone stood by and cheered us on.

With a face that had graced the cover of GQ magazine several times, he was fun, and I loved spending time with him. That made it easier to ignore the fact that we rarely had sex and that he lived with his hot 'uncle' in a fancy one-bedroom apartment in the West Village.

My drinking, bingeing, and purging escalated. There were nights Brynn and I would lock ourselves in the apartment, feasting on huge amounts of food we'd ordered from Sarge's Deli on 3rd Avenue. We called there so often that we knew the phone number by heart. They eventually stopped delivering to us because of all the checks we bounced.

I was crushed when Brynn told me we had to move out because her father was selling the apartment. "You're lying! You just want to get rid of me!" I screamed. A dark rage simmered deep inside of me as I trashed her apartment, smashing glass tables, and writing obscenities in lipstick on the bathroom mirror like a demon in a horror film.

I felt like a victim, alone and abandoned again. This time by an entire family. Years later, I discovered the reason Ike had sold the apartment was to move Brynn out of the city and into rehab in New Jersey.

Gimme! Gimme!

I met Anastasia on my European teen tour. We bonded in Italy when we poked holes in a fellow traveler's diaphragm with a pin. You could say we were the 'mean girls'. She also went to American University and ended up working at *Azul & Bleu* after she graduated.

After the whole Brynn debacle, she was a lifesaver when she suggested I move into her apartment on the Upper East Side. We made quite the team and off we went. With our oversized designer handbags, the pretentious bitches were on the loose.

My new drug of choice was diet pills, which enabled me to stay up almost all night. From Wall Street to Central Park, Anastasia and I took the city by storm. We threw parties, worked out at the hottest health clubs, hung out with the NY Rangers, and vacationed from Acapulco to Montreal. Not a stone was left unturned.

With our hair spritzed and gelled and sneakers on our feet, we put on our Sony Walkmen with Madonna blasting in our ears and trudged downtown to work together after just three or four hours of sleep.

On summer weekends, you could find us plotting or scheming our way into the best parties that were being thrown in The Hamptons or Fire Island. If we weren't there, you could find us either at her family's beach home on the Jersey Shore speeding around in her father's Porsche or at my parents' Country Club sipping Bloody Marys all day long, ringing up a bar tab for my parents.

I not only slept with her Uncle Evan, but I slept with four of her father's friends as well as I pranced about like Lady Godiva in my skimpy Norma Kamali bathing suits and funky Betsy Johnson outfits. I never got the memo that sleeping with your friend's relatives and her parent's best friends don't really mix.

Anastasia's father, Drew, was one of the most incredible men I've ever met. He had a heart of gold. Filled with an eternal zest for life, he hosted the best parties and barbeques and found no greater joy than in making his friends happy. His generosity knew no limits, and he never once judged me. I will always adore that man. He's now soaring high with the Angels and whenever I see a random balloon floating in the air, I'm sure Drew must have sent it to me from a party he's throwing in Heaven.

One day, I took it upon myself to wear Anastasia's diamond bezel gold Rolex watch. She was out of town and had the nerve to come back early. Why was that a bad thing? If I'd known she was coming back, rather than getting a mani/pedi, I would have slipped the watch back into her jewelry box.

That's why wearing it without asking her permission was basically stealing it. I never planned on keeping it, but how could I give it back without telling her what I'd done?

When she noticed it was missing, I denied taking it. A week later, I purposely dropped a jar of bubble bath powder that had been sitting on our bathroom shelf and buried the shiny gold Rolex inside the heaping pink mess on the floor. As if it had just levitated out of her room into the bathroom up onto the shelf, into the jar of bubble bath, and pushed itself off the shelf. Stranger things have happened, right?

I eventually told her the truth, which she'd known all along. She was gracious enough as a friend to forgive me and told me that all I had needed to do was ask her. She would have been more than happy to let me wear it. My ego and pride had kept me from doing that.

As if my life wasn't already filled with enough drama, I'd always been obsessed with soap operas. I watched the entire ABC lineup from 12:30 to 4pm and when I couldn't watch them—I taped them. (VCRs, another one of those 80s things). *The Edge of Night, All my Children, One Life to Live* and *General Hospital.* The Edge of Night was filmed in the City, only a few blocks away from *Azul & Bleu*, and I talked my way into the studio more than a few times. Anastasia ended up dating the ex-boyfriend of one of the show's major stars.

Michael E. Knight, who played Tad on *All My Children*, was one of the hottest and most popular guys on the soaps in the early 80s. I spotted him walking along the Upper West Side one afternoon and literally chased him and his girlfriend straight into the supermarket. So much for privacy.

After singing his praises, I mentioned I was a producer at *Azul & Bleu*, instantly promoting myself from secretary to producer. I then practically begged him for a tour of the studio for an imaginary project I was working on. He graciously gave me his number and told me to call him.

I was ecstatic when he arranged a tour for me and Anastasia, my 'assistant producer'. He introduced us to all the actors that were on set that day, including Susan Lucci, the queen of soaps herself. Still, I couldn't help but wonder, Why haven't any of my dreams come true yet? Why couldn't I have been a Soap Star?

I've always been extremely organized, which made me a great secretary. I liked my job, but I wanted MORE. So I was thrilled when the Creative Director I worked for promoted me to Junior Copywriter. I got my own office and my own Junior Art Director to work with. The thing is, I wasn't proving to be all that creative because I was more focused on my personal life than on my job. There was always a new guy for me to chase and when things didn't work out with him, I went back to Greyson.

Besides Anastasia's Rolex and half the male population of New York, I was obsessed with a bracelet I'd purchased at Ylang Ylang. Their pieces were ridiculously expensive for my budget, so when my bracelet broke, I made my own. I went downtown to the bead district and spent way more money on supplies than a new bracelet would have cost.

Consumed with making jewelry, I'd stay up till all hours of the night and even started selling my creations. Yet nothing filled the abyss inside of me. It suddenly dawned on me that if I got married, everything would be OK.

Not long afterwards, Greyson asked me to marry him. I knew that he'd always love me and I would always love him. He was my best friend and soulmate. No one ever made me laugh as much as he did. I have always loved him and I always will.

My parents threw us an engagement party. His sister threw me a surprise bridal shower. The engagement gifts started pouring in from Tiffany in their baby blue boxes and shiny white ribbons, and we flew off to Miami to start our new life together. The plan was for him to work in his family's ski and snowboarding resort business (because it's ALWAYS snowing here in tropical Miami) and for me to start my jewelry business which, in my mind, would be even bigger and better than Ylang Ylang. I would be a famous jewelry designer. We'd fly back to New York for a magnificent wedding at my parents' country club and live happily ever after.

Things didn't go exactly as planned. We got married, but I started cheating on him before the wedding. Nothing was ever enough for me.

LUV, BONNIE

LUV, BONNIE

Rainbow High

During the first year of my marriage, I spent a lot of time flying back and forth to New York to get supplies for my business. I designed jewelry, then had people help make and sell it for me. Some of my pieces even made it into a few stores in the prestigious *Bal Harbour Shops*. I was making some money, but I still felt empty inside.

Greyson and I were the first residents to live in our pristine, modern apartment up in the sky. An apartment like that would have been totally unaffordable in New York. It was on the 23rd floor and had the most incredible views over the water, city, and golf course. There were floor to ceiling windows in all the rooms and two huge balconies that captured both the sunrise and sunset. That's where I spent most of my days turning Swarovski Crystals into sparkling, wearable art pieces and watching soap operas. That, as I drank, binged and purged through the hours.

I'd binge for days on leftovers and end up in excruciating pain, my stomach blown up like a balloon. When I couldn't take it anymore, I reversed the cycle by starving myself for days. I'd wash down handfuls of diuretics with vodka or wine, to purge all the bloat and water weight I'd gained.

It was an endless, exhausting cycle. I'd end up

passing out before I had to pick up Greyson at work. I always had a joint waiting for him tucked inside my bra, which he pulled out with delight and smoked on the ride home.

Restless, irritable and discontent with everything, I became intrigued by the Mediterranean villas being constructed below. They were the first phase of the development, now known as *Acqua Blu*. I wondered if I could get a real estate license and sell them. I took the 1-week course to get my real estate sales associate license and passed the state exam within three weeks. It was intense, but worth it.

Willow, a sales rep for my jewelry line, had a brother named Wyatt, who was the project developer. What were the odds? She introduced us, and he hired me. The pre-construction site got very little traffic, and I was bored to death as I waited for people to come by. Now and then, Wyatt would whisk me away in his private jet for intimate business lunches. He always had lots of cocaine and alcohol on hand. A successful businessman (or so I thought), he owned a Porsche, a jet, and a gorgeous apartment in Coconut Grove, with stunning views of the Miami skyline.

Divorced for two years, he was now single (unlike me, who was still very married). I guess Wyatt was as distracted from his real estate project as I was from my impending jewelry empire because it went bankrupt before I even sold one villa. The corporation that eventually took over the project hired their own sales staff, and that was the end of my real estate career at *Acqua Blu*. It was also the end of Wyatt and me.

Greyson continued working while I toyed around with my jewelry, but it wasn't doing it for me. I craved excitement and maniacally hurling crystal wine goblets from our 23rd floor balcony into the parking lot below wasn't cutting it. I tried to distract myself and joined *The Spa at The Cielo Azul* in the renowned *Miami Beach Hotel.* Off I went every afternoon to my step aerobics classes in my matching tights, leotards, and leg warmers. Jane Fonda would have been proud.

I was quite the ball of energy after doing a bump of cocaine before leaving the house to curb my appetite and fire me up. After class, I'd stroll outside to the hotel's landmark pool, featuring a bar underneath a cascading waterfall. The sun, coupled with the aerobics, drugs and diuretics, wreaked havoc in my body and I was thirsty all the time. Why not have a cocktail? One or two drinks later, I'd head back inside and further dehydrate myself in the sauna. Perhaps I could lose a pound or two before heading back home.

Since drinking and driving 25 minutes to *The Cielo Azul* was risky, I joined the de *Luxe Spa at l'Océan,* which was just around the corner from our apartment. That's where I met Jeffrey, a drop-dead gorgeous podiatrist. A body to die for and deep emerald eyes that pierced straight through my heart. Our sex was out of this world and never one to differentiate between sex and love—I convinced myself I was in love with him.

I didn't want to be with Greyson anymore, but the thought of being alone terrified me. I'd come home after being with Jeffrey and lock myself in the bathroom, muffling my screams and tears into a towel, unable to look at myself in the mirror.

I stayed with Greyson and continued living a life of lies. I was lost. It was easier to blame him for my problems rather than taking a good look at myself and seeing that he wasn't the problem. I was.

The Doctor Is In

Every girl needs a good gynecologist. If for nothing more than your regular checkups. I found the best one in town. James Coopersmith, good ol' Jamie C.

Well, he was just the best doctor EVER. His eyes were like deep blue pools. He had a smile that brought out the sexiest dimples. He was a powerful Miami doctor, had a brilliant mind, and was just REALLY cute.

We flirted whenever I went to his office. Our flirting turned into a full-blown erotic affair. Whenever I called the office to talk to him, I called myself Lucky, referring to a character in one of my favorite Jackie Collins novels. There was endless passion between us, an insatiable fire that was dangerous and exciting. What I ignored was that he had a wife and a child.

Jamie reserved his after office hours for me. They were in the plush exam room where the D&Cs were performed. The nitrous oxide flowed as he thrust me down on the table. One minute he was stroking my face, then his rough hands were ravaging every part of my shaking body. We tumbled off the table and he'd hike me up onto the counter, my back pressed against the wall, him exploding like pop rocks in my mouth. Satisfied and exhausted, we emerged from the office.

We also spent days at the beach, drinking and having sex in our hotel room. Once we even had sex in the townhouse where he lived with his wife and son. They were selling it because they'd purchased a new home on Star Island where his wife spent most of her time decorating and overseeing the contractors.

I was green with envy. Why did SHE get the handsome, rich doctor and why was SHE going to have Don Johnson as her neighbor, living only a few houses away from where *Miami Vice* was being filmed?

Jamie didn't seem to mind being seen out in public with me. We'd cruise around in his white Lamborghini or grab lunch at *Carpaccio,* an alfresco café in the *Bal Harbour Shops.* I was terrified Greyson would see us, especially since he worked right there in the mall. Nothing like living on the edge, but I always made sure to have an excuse ready. Just in case. Like maybe I had cervical cancer and Dr. C wanted to take me out to lunch to soften the blow. Lies, lies, lies. I lied like it was nothing.

I had reached the point where I NEEDED more and more diuretics and I couldn't find doctors who would prescribe them to me anymore. I was tired of hearing that they weren't good for me and Jamie had reached the point where he wanted no part in having Gigi (his nurse, receptionist, and ex-wife) calling in scripts for me anymore. I couldn't help but wonder if he was sleeping with her, too, but I didn't really care. What did matter was that he told me how I could call them in on my own.

He informed me that the way to do it was for me to call the pharmacy and say that I was Gigi. I was unsure. "How can I do that? Don't I need a medical ID number or something?" Apparently not for something as harmless and non-addictive (for some) as diuretics.

Thus began an endless amount of calls to pharmacies all throughout the Miami area. I surely couldn't keep using the same pharmacy. Or pharmacies close to home where someone might recognize me. I didn't mind traveling to dilapidated high-crime neighborhoods to find an unsuspecting pharmacist.

I'd take a giant deep breath. My heart would race. Ring. Ring. OMG... "Hi!! This is Gigi from Dr. Coopersmith's office in North Miami. Our telephone number here is _____! Patient's name: Bonnie Salkow! Hygroten 100 mg! Number 100! (that would be the number of pills) Refills: 3!! Thanks so much!!" OMG, OMG, OMG! Yup, just like that.

The panic would set in all over again each time I drove up to the pharmacy to pick up the pills. *OMG, what if they call the police? I'm going to get arrested! OMG, OMG, OMG they're calling the police NOW! What's taking so long?!*

The pills would come, I'd pay, and the hysteria would continue all the way to my car and for about ten minutes afterward, certain that those cops were following me. Then finally, that HUGE sigh of relief once I realized that I'd gotten away with it. This time. Begging God, *Oh, please let this be the last time. I have to stop. I really have to stop this.*

Our affair ended. Years later, I learned I hadn't been the only one getting serviced after hours in Jamie's office. Whether he'd lost his medical license, one could only guess. But his gynecological practice closed, and he ended up going into the medical weight loss business and selling these magical cookies that supposedly melted off the pounds.

People started getting sick from the cookies. He was still eating the cookies, curbing his middle-aged belly that he no longer needed to get rid of with liposuction. Supposedly, it was heart failure, I'm not sure, but Jamie eventually passed away. He was only 52 years old, leaving behind his wife, child, and lots of uneaten boxes of cookies.

One Short Day

I'd been unraveling for some time and my life had become totally unmanageable. My potassium levels were depleted, there were bruises all over my body, I was weak, short of breath, and constantly on the verge of fainting. Day and night, I'd get these crippling pains in my hands and feet. As my body contorted, I made excruciating efforts to stop the cramping.

Racked with pain and out of my mind with terror, I was convinced, *I'm having a stroke. I'm having a heart attack. I'm going into kidney failure and I'm going to need dialysis*. I kept trying to stop taking the diuretics, but after a while, my fear of getting fat won out and I'd call in another script. When Greyson urged me to get help, I agreed to go to my first treatment center. *The Clover Institute for Eating Disorders.*

When the staff did my intake, they told me to consider that I was an alcoholic and drug addict. Now they were pushing it. True, I had never been able to control my drinking once I started. Yes, I was a blackout drinker. But I was here because of an eating disorder. "Are you going to help me with this or not?" I demanded.

My complaints were endless. "The food is disgusting. It's freezing here. Everyone here is fat.

Who does she think she is telling me what to do?" I was definitely not ready to surrender to a new way of life, so after 24 hours of being locked inside the clover patch, I was done. I called Greyson and he picked me up.

Regardless of being back in the comfort of my home, the grass was no greener here. I continued down the same path I'd been going on, which was leading me straight back to another dead end.

Delirious Escape

My next stop in Wonderland was *Crystal Bay Towers*, where I got a job leasing apartments. It was a three building community on the Intracoastal Waterway about two miles from home.

The maintenance supervisor of the property, Nikolas, looked like a Greek God. Married with four kids, he had a thing for Bazooka bubble gum. He must have chewed and popped more bubbles than all his kids combined. Everything about him popped.

By my third week at work, I was sneaking out of the leasing office and meeting him in empty apartments to have sex. The chemistry between us was electrifying. It was all fun and games until one day the manager had to do my job and show some apartments because I was nowhere to be found. Of all the empty units she could have chosen in three giant high-rise buildings, she chose the one Nikolas and I were in.

It all happened so fast. The faint rumbling of voices in the hallway turned into loud booming bursts of noise. Icy fear washed over us as Nikolas and I scrambled for our clothes. With our hearts pounding and bodies shaking, we threw ourselves across the room and out the door.

Luckily for us, the apartment was so big that the master bedroom we were in had its own exit door. We escaped the storm. Nikolas was hot, but he was a struggling family man with kids and, as thrilling as it was, it just wasn't worth the risk after that.

Nine months later, I decided it was time to move on. Again.

Written in the Stars

In retrospect, it's clear that the cards have always been stacked in my favor. I had a glorious life. I just never appreciated it. Nothing and no one was ever good enough for me.

I wanted to get another job working for a real estate developer and BOOM. In no time I was working on site for the developer of *Frizzante Baia Yacht Club*, a prestigious community of high-rise waterfront condos, townhomes and marina. Not in the safest neighborhood, but fully gated and known for its great security and award-winning landscaping. The developer was the former owner of Miami Beach's most legendary hotel. I viewed that as another impressive win for me because I was now hobnobbing with the crème de la crème of Miami Real Estate.

That's where I met Blaze. She was a barracuda. A force of nature. I still shudder at the sound of her heels marching down the hallway. Click, click, click, click, click. Her voice bellowing out our names to do this or to do that. Get this. Get that! Go here, go there. She was terrifying. But she taught me how to close a sale. "GET THAT CHECK", she'd boom. "You can't make a deal unless you get that check." I'll always be grateful to her for that.

I must have still had a thing for maintenance guys,

as I leaped into bed with Aiden, the head of the maintenance department, several times.

And I must have still had a thing for married men because I also found myself in bed with Myles, a well-known Miami defense attorney. Many an afternoon, I'd run off from the sales office with a handful of keys and disappear. We previewed lots of different apartments on the property, but he purchased none of them because he already lived there. With his wife and his three kids. But I knew that all along. He was like a life-sized candy apple. Forbidden, sweet, and delicious.

When most of the units were sold on the property, the sales office closed and it was time for me to find a new job. It was also time for me to get a divorce. Sadly, when my marriage to Greyson ended, so did my relationship with his family. It was an immense loss for me because one of the best things about being married was my new family. I'd known them since we were in college and I loved them all.

Greyson and I still speak, but I haven't spoken to anyone in his family since we split up. Even after our divorce, we continued to see each other. I still couldn't bear the thought of being alone, so I would go out on dinner dates while Greyson waited for me in my apartment to bring him home a doggy bag and have sex.

There were lots of dates, lots of trendy restaurants, and lots of dinners for me and Greyson, all compliments of my bevy of suitors. I have no doubt that Grayson and I are soulmates. Although we are apart, we will always be together.

Harbour

Puerto Seguro was a neighborhood restoration project nestled in South Beach with shops, restaurants, apartments and a park, all built around a world-class marina. It took about 20 years for it to become the trendy, beautiful enclave that it is today.

The original developer hired me to work in the sales office selling pre-construction units for the two luxury waterfront high-rise condos. It was to be the most beautiful and exclusive place to live on Miami Beach. All I needed to do was convince people they wanted to live there. Not an easy feat, as I was busy hiding in the bathroom, either bingeing on candy or chugging down vodka. I always kept a stash of both in my bag at all times. It doesn't get much messier than melted M&M's all over the bottom of your new handbag.

I sold a handful of units while I was there, one to a sweet guy named Channing. Sweet being the first problem. I slept with him and used him like an ATM. When I got bored, I dumped him.

When it came to interior design, Leonardo Z. was the biggest enchilada in Miami. With a striking resemblance to the Pillsbury Doughboy, he was a short and plump, fancy shmancy Jewish boy from Brooklyn, New York.

Leonardo, my ass. His real name was Lenny Zuckerman, but he'd built quite a reputation for himself. Since he had designed the model apartments for the sales office, he popped in a lot. Not shocking that we would start sleeping together, but we did.

One day, he surprised me with a beautiful diamond tennis bracelet and by the time the clasp had broken—the affair was over. I placed it in his hands, smiling sweetly. "Leonardo, can you please get this fixed for me? I can't believe it broke so quickly." Like I was ever going to see that bracelet back again. What nerve, I thought. That was a gift. How dare he not return it?

I thought it only right that his wife be called and informed that her cheating rat of a husband better return my tennis bracelet that he bought for me. I shudder to think how I ever could have done something so cruel to someone so innocent.

The developer and the head of the sales office were good friends with Leonardo Z. and his wife, yet I couldn't understand for the life of me why I got fired.

LUV, BONNIE

Man in the Mirror

I continued to blame the eating disorder for my problems because how many of these issues could I seriously tackle at once? This one was bad enough.

I couldn't just swallow a bunch of diuretics at the table if I was dining out with anyone, so I'd excuse myself and go to the ladies' room, open my bag, and pour out a huge handful of tiny white pills. God forbid one fell on the floor. I'd think, *Let's see how many of these I can fit into my mouth without me choking. Ten? Twelve? Fifteen?* I'd pop them in then scurry back to the table fast enough for the pills not to dissolve because that would have tasted vile.

Eyeing the table on my way back for my water glass, the first thing I'd do before I sat down was grab it. In the most ladylike way I could, I'd swallow them all down. No one would even know. Dare someone speak to me before I could find the water. Then what? I couldn't spit them out. *OMG, OMG! Where's that water!?* I'd think, frantically searching for my glass. Pause. Pause. Gulp. Gulp. "Oh, I'm so sorry! What were you saying? I was just so thirsty!"

Ace Recovery Center for Eating Disorders was the most renowned eating disorder treatment center in Miami, perhaps even the country. One of the owners, Tommy, was a handsome athlete and tennis aficionado with a doctorate in clinical psychology. He was also a recovering addict with a monumental ego and a successful business, with attractive young women running around the place with raging eating disorders.

I wanted to admit myself, but I didn't want to commit to long-term treatment. I've since learned that often what I think I want isn't always what I need. However, the Universe always has a way of conspiring to make things work out in our best interests.

Ace was an inpatient program, but there were some therapists available for those who wanted to be seen on an outpatient basis. Sick and tired of living in torment, I committed to the outpatient program.

I didn't have any significant interactions with Tommy when I was there other than in passing on my way to therapy. Brianna, my therapist, was required to report back to him and the rest of the treatment team regarding my weekly progress. I had set my sights on him and made it my mission to show up at all the 12-step meetings I knew he attended. Everyone knew I was enamored with him and he knew it as well.

"We need to keep this a secret," he said as soon as we began seeing each other. I didn't like it but went along with it, desperate to be with him no matter what the cost. He treated me like a stranger in public, but the sex was great and I didn't want to give THAT up. I gloated over the thought of his patients clutching their pearls with their mouths wide open, thinking, *If they only knew!*

Brianna suggested I refrain from dating anyone since I'd told her about my past obsessive relationships with men that often ended with me relapsing. I didn't listen to her and although I told her I was dating, I didn't tell her who it was. My bingeing and purging got so bad that I signed an agreement saying that if I continued bingeing, purging OR dating, I would commit to their long-term inpatient program. I signed the agreement with the rest of the staff, including Tommy.

I thought it ironic that the owner of an eating disorder treatment center who otherwise seemed to have an inflated ego had a ritual of staring at himself in the mirror, sucking in his stomach. "Do I look fat?" WHAT? If only your patients could see you, I thought. I was resenting him more and more because I felt like some dirty little secret. How long could I keep up this charade? My dreams of driving off together into the sunset in his shiny Jaguar were quickly disintegrating into smoke and ash.

He stopped returning my calls, and I became invisible to him. My bubble burst as he took off on his high horse. With each passing day, my anxiety and resentments grew and when I went back to therapy a few days later, I was seething, lamenting to Brianna about the breakup.

When she heard who HE was, she reacted as if I'd poured acid all over her. She tried to keep her composure throughout the rest of our session, but the next day I received a cursory call, letting me know yesterday had been our last session. I pleaded with her. "But what about long-term treatment? I need help! Are you all just going to abandon me?!"

Desperate and alone, I gulped down some vodka and a handful of water pills. I drifted off into a long dark tunnel where I begged God, *Please don't let me die. I promise I'll stop drinking and taking these pills. Please let me live.* When I opened my eyes, I called my friend Ryan. He took me to my first psych hospital and detox. I was dying. Physically, emotionally, and spiritually.

Ryan had a prosthetic arm. I'd never asked him the reason, because I assumed if he wanted me to know, he would have told me. As we drove to the hospital that day, he finally did.

After years of partying, he got behind the wheel of a car one night when he was high and totaled his car. That had been nine years before and he hadn't touched another drink or a drug since. It was no coincidence that I'd called Ryan when I did. We arrived with my Louis Vuitton handbag and luggage and after checking in (the nurse doing my intake), I perched myself on a chair and waited for the valet to take my bags to my room. There was no valet, and this was definitely not a hotel.

Dances at a Gathering

The iconic *Hotel California* by The Eagles has always been one of my favorite songs. It's remarkable how I can relate to so many of the lyrics. Like that 'Tiffany-twisted' mind. Who doesn't love a 'Mercedes Benz'?

I was fed up with amusing myself with all those 'pretty, pretty boys' who never wanted a relationship and only just wanted to be my 'friends'. Then there's the dancing. I've always loved dancing, especially a 'dance to forget'. I've always loved being complimented on my 'lovely face' but what about my body? Why wasn't that ever OK? How much easier it was to blame my body for all my pain than to face it.

'Pink champagne'? I always loved champagne. I loved pink and anything sparkly. Only who was I fooling thinking that I was 'living it up' with that lovely face of mine? Because every time I picked up a drink, no matter how pretty the color, all logic flew out the window and I became incapable of making any kind of rational decision.

'WE are all just prisoners here, of our own device.' What a comforting thought that I may not be alone after all. WE? Perhaps I wasn't the only one trapped inside my mind's prison. I speak from experience when I say that addiction is, without a shadow of a doubt, a FUCKING 'BEAST'. I can 'stab it' with as many 'steely knives' as I can find, but that thing just can't be killed. It enticed me, was impossible to resist, and landed me in 13 different treatment centers. Sure, I can 'check out' whenever I want. But I can 'never leave'.

I will ALWAYS be an alcoholic and addict. The great news is that I've learned that there is a way out. I can recover. One day at a time.

Come What May

My Louis Vuitton luggage would not keep me sober or take away the stabbing pain inside of me. To expect anyone to carry my bags, burdens, or 'stuff' will always be a serious mistake. Nobody can rescue me. I am the only one who is responsible for my recovery, wellbeing, and happiness.

I got a new therapist when I was dismissed from *Ace Recovery.* She'd known Tommy for many years. She urged me to report him to *the Department of Professional Regulation.* As far as she knew, I wasn't the only girl he'd done this to, so I reported him, not out of revenge, but because my therapist urged me to do so.

The truth of the matter is that he took advantage of a sick patient under his care when his job was to help and protect his patients. *Ace* closed and Tommy now owns another well-known treatment center in Florida. Everyone has their own path and as long as mine is clean, everyone else's is none of my business.

Losing My Mind

It wasn't long before I relapsed again, drowning in despair. I was admitted to a program called *Las Brisas at Bahia Bay* and that's where I met MAG, a Pop/Rock musical legend who was there recovering from his most recent slip.

When I first arrived, he stayed in his room most of the time with his door closed, the faint smell of alcohol seeping through the crack below. He hadn't used drugs in years and despite admitting that he was an addict—he thought it was OK for him to drink. He ended up in the hospital after overdosing on alcohol, otherwise known as alcohol poisoning. As many in recovery believe, and have painfully come to learn (including myself), alcohol IS a drug if you are an addict.

One day, he emerged from his room hugging his beloved guitar like a security blanket. Rough around the edges, with his mangled long blonde hair and bloodshot hazel eyes, he began earnestly singing one of his songs to a patient whose name was the same name as the song. Like he'd written it just for her. I couldn't have despised her more at that moment. Wasn't it bad enough that she was prettier than me, younger than me, and had a better body than me? Now he's SINGING A SONG TO HER? Did he like her MORE than me?

Locked inside and losing my mind, I raced up and down the hallways, huffing and puffing, breaking up the monotony with jumping jacks and sit-ups. You have to burn some more calories. My twisted mind kept telling me I couldn't just sit all day and not gain weight.

MAG stared at me in disbelief, shaking his head. He patted the chair next to him, motioning for me to sit down. "Why are you so worried? You're beautiful. My wife was a fucking goddess and I know real beauty when I see it." It was true, his wife was a multi-award winning singer, actress and star who was recognized all over the world for her beauty and talent. So if he told me I was beautiful, wouldn't that mean it was true? Wouldn't that make me OK? Not a chance. That can only come from inside—and I was an empty shell.

I was hell-bent on destroying myself. After my release from *Las Brisas*, I stumbled in and out of more treatment centers for drugs, alcohol, even sexual trauma. One morning, after yet another horrible night of drinking, I woke up trembling with the sweet taste of whipped cream in my mouth. I winced when I saw a guy I knew from college snoring beside me and jumped out of bed, trying not to slip on the whipped cream that was covering half the floor. I couldn't remember anything about the night before, but the whole thing was a sticky mess in so many ways.

The silver lining to that scare was that I immediately checked myself into the *Ohana Recovery Program,* where I was blessed with a miracle.

Something Wonderful

Slouched in chairs under the grim fluorescent lights, sat a group of despondent, bored and pissed off addicts trying to break free from the grips of their addictions. We were in the group therapy room at *Ohana.* Poised, tanned and rocking a pair of white stiletto heels (because everyone needs a pair of stilettos in rehab) I slunk through the room preparing to share my story. I beveled my long legs to display my new, polka dot hot pants, and pulled my shoulders back to show off as much cleavage as I could in my tight peplum top. With a toss of my long feathered hair, I placed my hand on my hip and took a deep breath.

"Hi, I'm Bonnie. I'm here because I have an eating disorder. I drink a lot, but alcohol isn't really my problem." The denial was incredible. Brent, one patient, remarked that I wasn't fat. Coyly batting my eyelashes, I threw him an appreciative glance. "Thank you, but you don't have to be fat to have an eating disorder."

I had to make sure that everyone in that room liked me, especially the men. Jon Jules and Hunter Stone were the co-owners of *Ohana* and, like most of their staff and all the patients, recovering addicts. I had the biggest crush on Jon, as did everyone else there. Not only was he stunning, with soft brown curls and baby blue eyes, but he had a smile that could light up the room like a burst of sunshine. He also had the best sense of humor.

Hunter was a burning beacon of raw sexuality. Everyone lusted after him, myself included. He referred to himself as the 'man with the golden arm', reason being that he'd shot so much dope into that gloriously muscled and tattoo covered arm, that it was worth its weight in gold. Both of them are soaring with the Angels now. Jon passed way too soon from cancer, while Hunter tragically overdosed. The beast of addiction never dies.

Brent was an easygoing spirit, an actor who had worked with some famous people in the industry but was here at *Ohana* because of his addiction to pain pills. Group work with him was very distracting. He was as delicious and hard as a piece of rock candy with his strong shoulders, ripped abs, and toned legs. We had great chemistry, but since he had a girlfriend, I settled for being friends with benefits. Years later, when he was married, I fell into the same dance...

Despite all the distractions, there was a camaraderie between us. We grew close over the nine months we were together and the primary focus was on our recovery. We wiped away tears and embraced our pain in group therapy sessions and tore apart our demons in individual therapy.

There were 12-step meetings and meditation groups. Roommates, we lived, cooked, cleaned, and went grocery shopping together. We worked out in the gym, strengthening our bodies and purging out the tension and pain from all the grueling therapy and emotionally exhausting work we were doing.

By the grace of God, after 17 years of abuse, I haven't touched a diuretic since the day I walked out their door. *The Ohana Recovery Program* has helped thousands of addicts and celebrities around the world and continues to do so. I have no words for how truly amazing the staff, my friends, and that entire experience was.

Carousel

So, what IS a binge? It's pure insanity.

Everything could be going great. I'm exercising every day, loving people, wanting to make plans and life's nothing short of wonderful. I'm grateful for everything. Life's a bowl of cherries. Cherries? Oh, no—I'm suddenly thinking about ice cream. Ice cream and pizza. I can think of nothing else until I get to them.

What flavor of ice cream should I get? I better get two or three pints because I can't decide. Plus a pizza. Also, a Boston cream donut and some salad with Italian dressing and some buttercream cake and lasagna and at this point it doesn't even matter. I just need to get MORE. They didn't even have the ice cream flavor I was originally craving, so I'm sure I will not be satisfied with all of this.

I'm probably going to come back tomorrow so I can get that ice cream flavor I wanted. What if they still don't have it? Will I just have to keep eating everything else until they get it? Once I get the ice cream I wanted, it's going to be something else I'm craving. Once I start this, nothing's ever enough.

Did I get enough food to last all day? There's nothing else I can focus on or accomplish because I'm so consumed with what I need to eat next. I'll eat in the car while I'm driving home and I may even need to stop at another store for more food. I'll plan what I'm going to eat first.

There's always lots of sugar, but I'll eat everything. From soup to nuts and then cookies and potato chips. Then ice cream and now I'm so full I need to pass out, but I'm too nauseous to even sleep. I keep eating and eating until my stomach feels like it's going to explode with the poisonous venom that transforms sweet Bonnie into a savage monster.

When I finally fall asleep without throwing up because that's the last thing in the world I want to do (GROSS), it's never a peaceful sleep because my stomach is still killing me. I wake up and eat some more. I'm in a total fog at this point and there's no way I can answer my phone or return any messages. My eyes are practically rolling back in my head and I can't move, but I'll force myself to get up off the sofa, shovel some more food into my mouth, and pass out again. Maybe I can watch some Netflix.

I force myself to finish every bite because tomorrow's a new day and I can start over, begin eating clean again. If there's absolutely no way I can finish everything, I'll throw out what I can't eat. I have to make sure that if I throw something out, it's destroyed. Maybe I'll pour lots of salt on top of the rest of the ice cream or pour lots of water all over the mac & cheese so I won't want to eat it. History has proven that anything in the garbage is fair game. It doesn't matter that the dog's wee-wee pads are in the trash. I'll dig out whatever food I can find and eat it.

Tomorrow comes and I still have those thoughts, so I have to do it again. Maybe it's the original ice cream flavor they didn't have that's haunting me. Perhaps it's a hamburger and french fries. Maybe it's Chinese food. Why did I throw out that food yesterday? Who was I kidding? I have to go out and buy more food. Enough to get me through the day.

Paranoia sets in the moment I step outside the front door. I'm certain that everyone is looking at me and thinking about how fat I am. I want bagels, but I'm too embarrassed to go into the bagel store because I'm afraid I might see someone that I know. *What would they think? I'm so fat,* that's all I can think about. *What can I eat next? Where can I go so that I'll see the least amount of people? Get in and out lickety-split with the food so I can return to the safety of my home and start eating everything.*

If it's the middle of the night and I need more food, I'll go down to my car and drive somewhere to get what I need. I want to get some candy out of the vending machine in the garage, but I'm afraid that people will see me. As if I were committing a crime and slashing someone's tires.

The shame is unbearable. I can't stand myself. I'm out of control, like a robot on a mission to destroy myself, but I don't care. The only thing I care about is what I can eat next.

I'll sneak food out of people's refrigerators when they're not looking. Rip open bags of cookies in the grocery store while I'm walking down the aisles because I can't wait until I leave the store to get that relief I crave so desperately for the entire world to slip away.

I once walked into *Williams Sonoma* during Christmas time and started picking away at their giant gingerbread house display. If they didn't want me to eat it, why did they bother to put it out?

My first sponsor, Victoria, once told me a great acronym for BINGE:

Because
I'm
Not
Good
Enough

It makes sense. When I binge, it's to not feel something (because I will eat until I feel nothing but physical pain) or to hurt myself. No one cares. I don't care—I want to die. I want to be thin. I want to be beautiful. I want to be younger. Better. I'm never good enough. So paranoid. So lonely. So terrified to leave the house. I don't want to feel whatever feelings I might be feeling. Filled with fear and shame. No one loves me.

I no longer shut the blinds but for years I would hide in the dark with the blinds drawn, shutting out not only the sunlight but the light of the Spirit of the Universe. Now when I go through one of these episodes, I know my Angels are always outside my window and as I look out at my beautiful view with all the boats and the people walking their dogs, living their lives, I just pray to be a part of the world again.

Now I need the light. No matter how dark it gets

inside my brain, I always want to see the light. I want to see it so badly. It could go on for days or weeks.

Then a switch flips and I seem to just pop out of the nightmare. I start again. I get up and shower. I go for a walk outside in the fresh air and sunlight. I call my friends. I never know how long I'm going to disappear for. When I'm in it, I feel like it's never going to end. Then, when I'm out of it, it feels like I'm never going to go back into the darkness.

Imagine being at a carnival, aimlessly wandering from one junk food stand to another. First you'll eat a churro. Then some nachos. You're wondering where the exit is. For God's sake, *WHERE IS THE COTTON CANDY?* You need to get out of there.

Kids are screaming and crying, people are bumping into you, everyone is chasing after their own dragons. Now it feels like you're dying of thirst and didn't you just pass a lemonade stand somewhere? Everything seems to spin and you just can't make it stop. It's like you're trapped in a dark cave with no end in sight.

As if by magic, you're suddenly swept out of that whole mess and you're standing in front of a beautiful carousel. You skip over to the prettiest pony you can find. You blissfully sit back and relax on your pony as the ride begins. Your body sways up and down and sweet music calms your soul. You're surrounded by pastel-colored horses covered in sparkles and gold. You're feeling happy and free at last.

Suddenly, the ride comes to a halt. That was way

too soon. You weren't ready. What happened? You were feeling so good. Why do you have to get off? When did it get so dark? Why did the music stop? Filled with dread, you step off the carousel and slip on a half eaten hot dog with mustard smeared all over the ground, as the joy is sucked right out of you, being driven back to the churro stand by some force that you can't control.

Newsies

One of my closest friends from *Ohana*, Joey, had been living alone in a large home on the bay in Keystone Point before treatment. Magnificent, yes. But it was basically empty. He'd been meaning to get around to renovating it, but got sideswiped by his addiction. Isolating is never a great idea, especially for an addict, so when we left *Ohana*, he invited me to move in with him.

My bedroom was on one side of the house and his on the other. We've remained great friends to this day, and I doubt that would have been the case had we slept together.

I was encouraged to get a stress-free job so that I could work on myself and my recovery. This meant getting a sponsor and working the 12 steps of the program. As grateful as I was that I wasn't using diuretics, drugs or alcohol, recovery still wasn't my chief priority. The meetings I attended were more of a social thing for me and I was still searching for that great guy to fix me.

I got a job as a receptionist answering the phones and booking appointments in an avant-garde hair salon in *The Bal Harbour Shops*. The only stressful part of the job was worrying what people would think if they saw me working there.

I didn't feel any sense of gratitude for being welcomed into this beautiful environment with a talented team of stylists and makeup artists.

Two avid soccer playing brothers from Argentina, (spicier than any dish you could imagine), owned the salon. With silky shoulder length hair and bodies that were as chiseled as their faces, they were stunning. Although one was married, what transpired in the bathroom with the two of them and the wealthy ladies who pranced through the mall was nothing short of scandalous.

Stella began her career at *Boyd's Madison Avenue*, the world-famous beauty apothecary, adored by some of the most famous faces in Hollywood. She had done makeup for Diana Ross, Liza Minnelli, and lots of other celebs, models and socialites.

She now had her own line of skincare and cosmetics, and Miami's 'elite' would come into the salon to have Stella do their makeup for special events, pop in for facials, or just to buy some of her fabulous products. Not long after I started working there, she asked me to be her assistant.

I loved working with Stella. She taught me how to do her rare technique of makeup application and how to do proper facials. I repaid her by stealing from her, hoping she wouldn't notice all the makeup and supplies missing because of the huge inventory she kept. I felt entitled to take whatever I wanted, but I took nothing she didn't have at least nine of in stock. Surely, I thought, I needed them more than she did.

One day, this arrestingly beautiful guy walked into

the salon, sending waves of heat through my body. Stella knew him and I was thrilled when she suggested I give him a facial. His name was Michael, and Stella told me he was a sports reporter for one of the major local stations.

We flirted all throughout the facial as I traced my fingers across his face and neck and gently inhaled his sweet, minty breath. All I wanted to do was rip his clothes off. After the facial, he asked me for my phone number. I sold him some products and sent him on his way. I was drawn to him like a magnet, not only because of the physical attraction, but because he was a local celebrity as well.

Michael wined and dined me. To be exact, there was no wine since he was also in recovery! He showered me with flowers, cards, and gifts. I was absolutely crazy about him, crazy being the operative word to come.

Never having had an interest in sports before, I suddenly couldn't wait to watch the news. Few people had cell phones, and beepers were the trend at the time—and an annoying one at that. The minute he went live, I'd start beeping him. My 'presence' was live on TV, so wasn't I practically on TV, too? Sort of? One step closer, at least, to being a star?

There was a small catch with this situation. Michael was married, although he was adamant that his marriage was over. They were officially separated, not living together, and just waiting to finalize the details of the divorce. I thought this was IT. How could it NOT have been? When I was with him, I felt beautiful and sexy. Our personalities fit as perfectly as our bodies.

He would pick me up at Joey's after work around 11:30 or midnight, and I'd be dolled up and waiting for him. Sometimes we'd go out before he went on air for a bite to eat or a romantic drive along the beach, convertible top down, pants off. We'd have mind-blowing sex on his balcony, staring out at the moonlit ocean as people strolled along the boardwalk below.

Then, as if a bomb had exploded, shards of glass ripped through my heart when he told me the news. "My wife's pregnant." What? OMG. "With twins." OMG. I wonder how that could have happened.

I was heartbroken. I swore I'd never go out with a man again unless he was divorced, because being separated obviously didn't mean a thing.

Michael's career exploded, and he got a job hosting a national TV sports show. Several years later, when I'd relapsed, I called him from a sushi restaurant one night. I was a drunken mess. Surely, by now, he's got to be tired of his wife, I hoped.

No such luck. He was thrilled with his new family. Dammit. Why does everyone else get to be so happy? In no condition to drive, Michael offered to drive me home. Devoid of all self-respect, I began unbuttoning my shirt, and he stopped me. I was filled with shame, but I still couldn't stop drinking.

Maybe a nose job would fix me, I thought. The obsession with that perfectly upturned nose had never left me. Nor had my unrelenting resentment towards Michael. Pouring more salt into that wound, I called him out of the blue one day and told him that if he didn't give me the money to pay for my nose job, I would call his wife and tell him we were having an affair. Blackmail. Everything was all about ME. It didn't matter who I hurt to get what I wanted.

Beyond My Wildest Dreams

Villagio del L'Acqua was a magnificent waterfront development owned by two well-known Miami real estate developers, Frederick Cohen and Barney McDonald, (better known as Fred and Barney, yes, like the Flintstones). Greyson, my ex, was friends with Fred and when he introduced us, I was hired on the spot.

His name was Chase, and he was as surprised to see us when I opened his door as we were to see him. I gasped as I flung myself back into the hallway. "Oh, I'm so sorry! I didn't know anyone was home!" There he stood, mopping water off the floor, wearing nothing but a pair of plaid boxers. My face flushed as I tried to catch my breath, unable to keep my eyes off him as I explained my presence. "The showing instructions indicated it wasn't necessary to call before entering the unit because we thought the owners were out of the country."

Chase, the owner's son, had flown in on the red-eye flight the night before from California because of a ceiling leak in the apartment and he forgot to notify the sales office that he was in the apartment. He had this sweet boyish charm and no idea just how good-looking he was. He apologetically shrugged his glistening shoulders. Awkwardly stepping aside, he reached for his mop and grabbed the bucket of water and invited us into the unit with a radiant smile. Now I really couldn't breathe.

In a trance, I showed my clients around the apartment, which was filled with beautiful decor, magnificent artwork, and photos scattered about of the owners posing with a bunch of different celebrities and icons. *Who was this guy?* I wondered.

The most captivating thing in the room, by far, was Chase. He had a striking resemblance to a young Dean Cain (Superman) as well as a young Elvis Presley. Intelligent, funny, friendly and sincere, he was a smoldering vision with eyes as dark as night, skin bronzed to perfection, and straight silky hair that begged you to run your hands through it. There was nothing he didn't have. Except me. YET.

I left my business card on the kitchen counter and was over the moon when he called to ask me out. We got along famously. One date led to another and then another, and that led into a three-month whirlwind of adventure and romance. He swept me off my feet. It was unbridled passion from the moment I laid eyes on him.

We set our imaginations free, making colorful clay animals together in a pottery studio. At *Dave and Busters,* he loved playing video games so he could win stuffed animals for me, then jump up and down with excitement. We'd go back to my place, and he'd roll around on the floor with Coco, my Maltese, with the little wind-up toy he gave her. We went to *Marlins Games* and kicked back in the sun, sharing pretzels and hot dogs.

Everywhere we went, he made new friends, speaking to them in their language if he knew it. I could have stared at him for hours watching him cheer on the Dodgers, his favorite baseball team. Only a few years younger than me, Chase was a joyful child at heart, and his enthusiasm for life was contagious.

We took lots of photos, made funny faces, and we laughed all the time. We spent hours in bed singing theme songs from TV shows we remembered from when we were kids. When we weren't laughing, we were making love. Everywhere and anywhere. His body was built for pleasure. His lips were luscious and his kisses were like chocolate that melted in my mouth. Time stood still when we were together.

Clinging to his every word, I listened as Chase entertained me with stories of his travels and romps around the world. His mother, Jade, an exotic beauty, was the leading actress on a popular 1960s TV sitcom. Her husband Jasper, as modest as he was, was of royal descent. The two of them spent a lot of time traveling around the world and entertaining on their yacht, *Pink Jade.* Hence, the photos in the apartment.

Despite living a life of luxury, Chase couldn't have been more down-to-earth. He said he'd produced some films I'd never heard of, but what did it matter? He spent his life drinking in all the beauty that life offered and now he was choosing ME to do it with. I drank very little when we were together because I didn't need alcohol when I was with him. HE was my addiction. I was happy as long as I had him by my side.

Chase was a Gemini, and if you know nothing about Geminis, know that they need to roam. He'd only intended to stay in Miami for a few days, but we were so caught up on our adventure that he didn't want to leave. "I need to fly back to California for my cousin's wedding this weekend, but I promise I'll be back soon," he said, assuring me he loved me. My mood plummeted. We'd been living a fairytale romance, and I didn't want to go back to reality and life without him. But he had to go.

When he first left, I squealed with joy every time I received his flowers, love letters, and daily phone calls. But that wasn't enough for me. I began drinking a lot and became increasingly distant and irrational with each call. My fears and insecurities got the best of me and despite his efforts to reassure me, I was convinced that he didn't want to be with me anymore. "I thought we were going to travel together. When can I come and visit you?" I pressured him.

I'd get blackout drunk, throw tantrums, and have no recollection the next day of what I said to him the night before. My behavior took a toll on him, hurting him a lot. I couldn't see it at the time because all I could see was how he was hurting ME by not wanting to drop everything, be with ME, and live happily ever after. When he told me we needed to take a break, I was shattered. I begged and pleaded with him, but all my efforts were in vain.

I screamed, cried, and lashed out at the world. But the one I hurt the most was myself.

LUV, BONNIE

LUV, BONNIE

Wicked

The first time I saw Wiley was at a Sunday evening 12-step candlelight meeting I used to go to. He drove a red Ferrari, was dressed in white Versace linen from head to toe (his signature look) and had long dirty blonde hair. Oh, yes, and a perfect ass. Turned out, not only did he have one but could often be one with that Napoleon complex of his. Yet I crushed on him the moment I laid eyes on him.

After losing my job at *Villagio del L'Acqua*, I went to work with Wiley in his real estate office, *Travertine Investments*, which turned out to be a brilliant move. Our offices specialized in luxury property sales but branched out into property management and rentals over the years. Agents came and went like flies, but the ones that stayed for a while became like family. I had the best of times and the worst of times there.

I was one of the top agents in the office who specialized in rentals. Handling a rental was a piece of cake. You'd just walk your client into three or four different rental communities and they'd choose the one they liked the best. The agents in the rental communities did all the work while I went straight into the kitchen and ate the frozen cookie dough they stored in the freezers to make cookies for the clients. When the client moved in, our office would get paid either a month's rent or a flat fee, sometimes as much as $1,500.

I became friendly with the leasing agents at the various properties around town (especially the properties that served those cookies) and several agents would then attach my business card onto their guest's registration card, despite me not even knowing who the guest was. I'd make a commission and split it with the leasing agent.

I could have lost my real estate license, or worse, gone to jail, not that the idea worried me too much. Wiley knew what I was doing and wasn't concerned because he was making money from the transactions too. I was logging in up to three rentals a day and to everyone in the office—I looked like a superstar! Although, who was I kidding? I was just a thief.

Over the nine years I worked at *Travertine Investments,* I slept with three of my co-workers, all of whom were working there at the same time. There was Billy, a sweet-talking gambler and a doofus of sorts with a body to die for. Originally from Turkey, he stood over six feet tall and, like a giant piece of Turkish Taffy, was melt-in-your-mouth delicious. He'd bring in a six-foot hero sandwich for lunch every day and devour the entire thing right at his desk. Who wouldn't want a bite of that?

Then there was Eric, a clean cut, rigid intellect who pinched pennies and would eat a tub of salsa and smelly tuna every day at his desk. Like anyone needed to smell that. He was an avid runner, slim and athletic, with a body as hard as a rock. My favorite times with him were grabbing frozen daiquiris at *Wet Willie's* in South Beach, having sex in their bathroom, then heading out to the beach for a tan.

Then there was kinky Peter. Peter Peter Pumpkin Eater didn't so much love eating pumpkin as he did feet. "When you get your pedicure, save all the scraps for me." Ewww, I know. One of the best times we had was a fun-filled trip to Vegas with Wiley and his wife Sierra, who'd become my best friend. We mostly shopped while Peter gambled. He passed soon after that trip and he's most likely playing '21' with the Angels now and polishing their toenails.

Small World

Now and then, I'd get together with Brynn, who was living with her Grandma Eden until she met and married Daniel. After I trashed our apartment in New York, Brynn's father sent her to that rehab in New Jersey, and she's been sober ever since—over 36 years! She's a walking miracle.

Her husband Daniel was a criminal attorney who, with Brynn's support, fulfilled his lifelong dream of becoming a judge. His eyes lit up when he looked at her. Her life turned around when she got sober and although I was still an absolute mess, she was very supportive of me.

One summer day I stormed out of the office after having a huge blow-out with Wiley, which happened often. I visited Brynn at her new house, which was only about a mile from the office. With my sundress clinging to my skin, I trudged there in the 90 degree heat and humidity, refreshing myself along the way with apple juice that I'd spiked with vodka.

I finally stumbled into her house, dripping with sweat and leaving a trail of mini vodka behind me. I always wonder what the story is behind all those tiny empty liquor bottles you see in the streets. You notice you only see the mini ones? Is it an alcoholic thing just to fling them away when you're done?

Brynn and Daniel were knee-deep in renovations. You could hear contractors banging and slamming and yelling from every room. I waved a quick hello to Daniel, who was floating on a raft in the pool as Brynn and I ducked into the guest bedroom. We grabbed a couple of paint brushes, opened up a jar of paint, and started splattering bright yellow paint all over the closet.

One thing led to another and next thing you know, I couldn't believe what I was hearing.

Brynn had talked about her Uncle Jon and his family for years, but I'd never paid too much attention to what she or anyone else said unless it was about ME. This time, however, I did a double take. "Did you say Uncle Jon owns a treatment center? In Miami?" OMG, OMG Could it be? "Is the name of the treatment center, *Ohana*?" Sure enough, her answer was a resounding yes. OMG, OMG... Jon from *Ohana*, the one I had a crush on for all those years, was UNCLE JON! What were the odds?! What a small world.

I never made it back to work that day and we never finished painting the closet. Brynn still lives in that house and loves the half splattered paint look. Go figure.

Over the Rainbow

My co-worker Paisley was a real firecracker. She came to Florida and got her real estate license after years of working in New York's garment center. Quite the fashionista, she paraded in one day wearing this striking navy blue Donna Karan cardigan with pearl buttons. She told me it was straight off the showroom rack and was only one of a handful that had been made. "This is no ordinary sweater," she boasted.

Paisley did lots of rentals and gave me a run for my money. I glared at her with each new one she did. *That bitch will not take away my spotlight!* I muttered to myself. The competition annoyed me. She was harsh and rattled off her opinions, but underneath it all, she was very likeable. We were both originally from New York, loved to drink like fish, and would jump through hoops to get Wiley's attention. In fact, she even went as far as cutting a rival real estate office's phone lines just to appease him.

One evening, Coco and I went to South Beach to meet her. As we relaxed on the balcony, sipping drinks and watching the skyline turn crimson, Paisley yanked Coco from me and dangled her over the balcony. My heart stopped. Coco swayed back and forth as I gasped for air. My heart pounded violently in my chest. With trembling hands, I pulled Coco back into the safety of my arms. Paisley contemptuously laughed the whole thing off. At this point I should have gone home, but since all reason had flown out the window after I'd started drinking, we got into her car and went off in search of food.

After ordering dinner, Paisley (already loud at this point) popped a few pills and disappeared. A waiter appeared with an expensive bottle of champagne. I raised an eyebrow. "Where did this come from?" I asked. "She ordered it," he said, pointing to Paisley who was winding her way back to the table.

She sat down, leaned over and whispered her plan to sneak out without paying for dinner or the champagne. I was having no part of it, so I signaled for the check, paid my share of the bill (not including the champagne) and darted out of the restaurant. I left her sitting alone at the table with her food and champagne.

I was jolted awake at 3am by the phone ringing. It was Paisley, barely comprehensible. "WHERE DID YOU GO? I'm in jail. The cops beat me up. They have my car. I need to get out of here." Guilt engulfed me as I paced back and forth in a state of panic. She was released the next day but, because of some other pending legal issues, was sent back to jail.

Apprehensive about seeing her, I swallowed my feelings and went to visit her. Inside the jail, there are signs all around saying that if an inmate threatens to harm themselves or anyone else, you need to report them. Just being inside a jail would make anyone distraught. So I didn't give it much thought when she said that she was going to kill herself as soon as she got out because she'd threatened to kill herself countless times before she was even sent to jail.

The judge took mercy on her and sent her to rehab rather than keeping her in jail, even though she scoffed at the idea that she had a drinking or drug problem.

Foxy's Place, in downtown Miami, is a hardcore drug and alcohol treatment center where most patients were court appointed, homeless, or living on the streets selling their bodies for a hit of crack. No one was getting served green smoothies or taking yoga classes there. It was also highly unlikely that any of the patients had the vaguest idea who Donna Karan was.

Paisley was a ball of fire, but that fire was rapidly turning into cinders. I received a call from her one day and she was frantic. She felt persecuted by 'those addicts' and livid at not being allowed to dye her gray roots, wear leggings, or makeup. I listened to her shrieking outburst as she begged me to pick her up and let her stay at my place. Her state of mind scared me and an icy chill went through my body. I had a feeling that she may even show up at my building.

Then came the tragic phone call from Sage, Sierra's sister, who also worked with us. "Bonnie! Turn on CNN! Now!" There, before my eyes, was Paisley magnified on my TV screen, dressed in her orange prison jumpsuit with her bright red hair and gray roots.

Frozen, with my hand over my heart, I started shaking as I listened in shock. My friend's body had been discovered outside *The Hamilton on the Bay*. Her body was so mangled and unrecognizable that it was suspected she had fallen out of an airplane. That wasn't the case. Paisley had left treatment, made her way up to the roof of *The Hamilton on the Bay*, and jumped 40 stories to her death.

A rush of emotions flooded through me. It was the first time I'd experienced a friend committing suicide. Anger, sadness, frustration, helplessness were all feelings I grappled with. I reminded myself that I wasn't responsible for what happened. Her problems started long before that fateful night in South Beach.

Just a few days later, Paisley came to me in a dream and let me know she was at peace. That same week, I walked into a thrift store and found that rare navy blue Donna Karan sweater with the pearl buttons. I know it was a gift from Paisley and trust that she's at peace now with the Angels.

Cell Block Tango

I'd first seen Mason in the 12-step rooms but barely cast a glance in his direction. One day, he strolled into our office looking for a place to live, holding hands with a blonde woman and a little girl. Another agent in the office helped them and I didn't see him again until I bumped into him at a meeting. His knee brushed mine as he slid into the chair next to me and leaned in. "Colby and I broke up, and I moved out," he said. Apparently, Colby was the blonde he was with in my office and the little girl was HER child, not his.

We went out a few times. His tanned sculpted body got my heart beating but his face, lack of ambition and unimpressive job had me pulling back. Yet there was something about the sweet smell of his coconut body wash that kept pulling me back in. How harmless could it be to sleep with him? So I did. Just like that.

Not long afterwards, I got a call from Mason. "I need to speak with you and it can't wait." I wondered what could have been that important, that he had to tell me the night of the season finale of *Melrose Place*? (TV's hottest show at the time was filled with more sex, scandal and drama than my own life and I was obsessed with it) My head spun as thoughts raced through my head, What if he has an STD? What if all my sleeping around had finally caught up to me?

OMG. I agreed to meet with him.

The big announcement was that he was back together with Colby. That wouldn't have been the biggest deal if Colby was his ex-girlfriend. The thing is, she was his WIFE. That's when I lost it. I didn't even LIKE him that much, SLEPT with him and then he BREAKS UP with me a few days later to get back with not his ex-girlfriend... but his WIFE?!

My friend Elizabeth, who also was the leasing manager of *Corsi d'Acqua*, the building I lived in, loved to party as much as I did. Still reeling from Mason's news, I called her and she came right over. While downing a bottle (or two) of wine, I gave her the update. The two of us put our drunken heads together, made a plan, then marched out the door to carry it out.

When we arrived at their apartment and saw both of their cars, things got out of hand. We staggered through the parking lot like hunters stalking their prey. I dug my keys into the side of Mason's car, and Elizabeth keyed Colby's car. We made quite a ruckus, giggling and howling with laughter. I dropped my keys, nearly tripped over them, but we got away before the cops arrived.

When I woke up with a not-so-surprising hangover and guilty conscience to match, I left a message on Mason's phone apologizing and offering to pay for the damage I did to his car.

He didn't reply to my message, but a few days later, there was a knock on my front door. I thought it was Sage coming to pick me up because we had plans to celebrate her birthday. The festivities were going to have to wait because upon opening the door—I came face to face with two police officers.

There was no denying what I'd done. "We heard the phone message you left for Mason." Dammit. After being advised of my Miranda rights, I was given the choice to exit the building peacefully or to continue arguing with them and leave in handcuffs. I chose the peaceful route, as did Elizabeth, who got whisked away from her job next door in the leasing office.

Off we went to jail, our next adventure. Not a fun one. An adventure filled with bologna sandwiches, humiliation, loss of rights, privacy and personal property while being locked up with no fresh air or sunlight. Not to mention getting photographed, fingerprinted, and body-searched.

Even though I got bailed out after four hours, I'd never felt so grimy. I peeled off my foul-smelling clothes and immediately jumped into a scathing, hot shower. The soapy water pouring through my hair and down my body was delightful. Sweet freedom whispered in my ear and not fifteen minutes later, I was out the door meeting Elizabeth for drinks, ingesting the same poison that sent us to jail.

What's the definition of insanity? Doing the same thing over and over, expecting different results. It took me many more years to learn that I cannot drink like normal people.

My crime was considered a felony based on the value of Mason's car and the damage that I created.

Besides my attorney's fees, I was ordered to make financial restitution and mandated to attend an 8-week anger management class, where I learned that most people in jail are there because of crimes committed while under the influence of drugs or alcohol. Luckily, I was able to have everything expunged to avoid having a criminal record, but it will never be expunged from my mind.

Money, Money, Money

Despite making a decent living, I never seemed to have enough money. Cory was a real estate broker I met while showing one of his properties, a waterfront townhouse in Eastern Shores. That's where I plucked a ripe crystal Steuben apple right off the dining room table that I ended up selling on Ebay. I never seemed to have ENOUGH of anything. I needed MORE clothes, MORE bags, MORE shoes. It was always something.

Cory was also, one could say, a high-class pimp (if there even is such a thing). He asked if I was interested in making some extra money by hanging out with some of his friends. Just some dinner, maybe a Miami Heat game, no pressure at all. "Some of them you wouldn't even have to sleep with." *What could be so bad?* I thought. So I took him up on his offer. He would usually even pay me in advance. How's that for trust? A trusting realtor/pimp. Quite a rare find.

His first friend (how surprising that his name wasn't John) was looking for a new piece of arm candy to bring to a Miami Dolphins game and dinner in Bal Harbour afterwards. According to Cory, if I was lucky, there'd be more dates to follow. I didn't mind being a guinea pig because the money was good and I imagined myself in between the game and dinner, flitting from store to store in the *Bal Harbour*

Shops getting lots of presents and digging a hole straight through his pocket.

I yawned throughout the football game. There was no pre-dinner shopping, and I ended up yawning through the entire dinner as well. Since there were no gifts, I wasn't about to transform myself into a bunny, so there was no sex and no second date. The money was good, so I reluctantly agreed to meet another one of Cory's friends.

This one was a Hasidic Jew whose name I'll never be privy to. That was evidently top secret information and this mission, that I accepted, differed from the last. Perhaps a blow-up doll would have been more suitable for him.

I was instructed to go to his penthouse apartment on the beach and told that the front door would be open when I arrived. Laser focused on my assignment, I gave my name and the guy's unit number to the hostile concierge at the front desk. *Did he have any idea how my feet were killing me in these new shoes? Did he even care?* After having me sign the guest register, it was time for me to go upstairs.

I squirmed the entire elevator ride up to the apartment with what had to be the last uniformed elevator man left on Miami Beach. While strutting out of the elevator in my new 5-inch heels, I wondered how many other pairs of stilettos this elevator man had heard CLICK, CLICK, CLICKING down the cold marble hallway? I arrived at the apartment with blisters on my feet, twisted open the doorknob, and hobbled into the barren apartment.

A tiny piece of paper with my name on it was propped up on a table. Scribbled on the note were explicit instructions for me to disrobe on a huge white sheet in the living room, face the window, and wait for him to come into the room. I was NOT to look at him and I was to stare out the window the entire time he was in the room. Mr. Mystery Man grunted as he did me from behind, pawing me with his clammy hands and thrusting his filthy load inside me after two revolting minutes. With ice running through his veins, he commanded, "Get dressed and take the money on your way out. And don't look back at me." How demeaning.

Next on deck was York, a well-known news anchor. If my self-esteem was bad before, hanging out with Cory's lotharios had plunged my self-worth to a whole new level of low. I heard his TV blaring as I made my way down the hall in my black lace jumpsuit and my new Carlos Falchi handbag, ready to take flight to the nearest disco. I pushed my ear up against the door and made out the sounds of a football game. Fun. I knocked on the door. "The door's open!" Cautiously opening the door, I peered inside.

Sprawled across the sofa in all his glory, York was wearing stained baggy shorts and nothing else. He was quite a sight to behold, with bloodshot eyes and three thick fat rolls of pale jiggly stomach. White powder was speckled across his face as saliva drooled from the side of his crusty mouth. Hey, buddy, no need to get dressed up for me.

He was zonked out of his mind, but I was just happy that he was focused on the game and the plate full of cocaine piled in front of him rather than on me. So I made my way into the kitchen and dug out a bottle of vodka from his freezer.

I crept into the bathroom with my bottle and eventually passed out on the floor while he snorted more blow in the living room. The BANG, BANG, banging noise of his fists pounding on the door shook me awake. Nauseous and lying there with a massive headache, I needed an escape plan. It was crystal clear that this dreamy snowflake wanted me to star in his own halftime show. He was definitely looking at the wrong Ice Princess. No way was this guy coming near me.

In the blink of a blizzard, I grabbed my bag, blew out the door, and never looked back. I was done with finding a Sugar Daddy. The morning after, I called Cory and told him I was done. I was disgraced. Using people for ANY reason isn't good. Good Lord, my life was in ruins.

Consider Yourself at Home

I first met Maxie, a neighbor at *Corsi d'Acqua*, while I was out walking Coco. We clicked instantly.She had three pugs—the 'Three Little Puggies'. Theo, her fiancé Dunkin's favorite, mischievous Ben, who'd chew everything from razor blades to food scraps, and Mickey, the sweetest little sugar plum.

Coco and I spent lots of time at Maxie and Dunkin's apartment, engulfed in their love. When we weren't there, we were out and about exercising or shopping, trekking through the mall for hours on end. "I can't believe it's dark out already," we'd say, as we shoved our packages into the back of Maxie's Jeep.

At home, she had trinkets, clothes and treasures stuffed into boxes, drawers and closets all over the apartment and was more than happy to let me sift through and organize everything. I LOVED organizing and Maxie loved collecting things and throwing them around.

We laughed until our sides hurt and shared our deepest, darkest secrets. She wasn't much of a drinker, but never minded that I drank myself into oblivion. I could never afford to buy as much as her, but I ran as fast as I could to keep up, charging up enormous debt on my credit cards. I suppose I could pawn my watch again, I reasoned.

As the bills piled up, panic set in, and fear loomed over me until I couldn't take it anymore and went to my mother. *This will be the last time*, I'd tell myself, bracing myself for another round of my mother's fury. "Mom, I need more money." Inches away from my face, she'd start screaming. "DIDN'T I JUST GIVE YOU MONEY?" Shaking with fear, I'd wipe the spittle off my face. "I don't give a shit if you have to sell your body for money. This is the last time I'm giving it to you." (I guess she hadn't received the news that I already HAD sold my body for money). She reached into her handbag, pulled out the checkbook, and wrote me another check. I cowered away.

There were days I'd go to Maxie and Dunkin's just to soak in the safety and comfort of their home. Surrounded by the four dogs, I'd turn on the TV and sink down into their comfy down comforter, snuggle and play with the dogs that got buried in between the softest pillows I'd ever felt. Despite being only ten years older than me, Maxie was the nurturing mom I'd always wanted.

Maxie had two children from her previous marriage, Alec and Ali. I envied how close she was to Ali. It never ceased to amaze me when a mother and daughter were so close. *Why can't I have a mother like Maxie?* I pouted to myself, always wanting what someone else had.

Ali had an apartment in New York, one in Miami, and tons of designer bags, shoes, and clothes. I was filled with envy. It wasn't enough for me to have a friend that loved me and included me in her family dinners, birthdays, and holidays. One that let me borrow anything I wanted and trusted me implicitly with the key to her home. Her friendship was the best gift of all. Yet I betrayed it.

Coco and I often stayed at Maxie and Dunkin's place whenever Maxie went to their other home in Key West. Dunkin spent most of his time there, since he owned a small chain of *Joe and the Beanstalk* cafés in the Keys. I'd putter around their apartment at *Corsi d'Acqua* like I was at *The Ritz Carlton*, sleeping in the Princess in the Pea Bed, watching TV, rummaging through Maxie's closets and drawers, and exploring and rearranging all her STUFF.

One day, while on one of my digs, I became obsessed with a Hermes scarf I found, the collectible Doll Scarf. I'd owned nothing Hermes before and here was this luxurious silken treasure in the softest shades of pastels, lost in the back of the closet. Surely Maxie wouldn't notice it missing amongst the endless sea of gems? My greed consumed me and I took it.

She mentioned the scarf was missing about a week or two later. I took a deep breath, trying to remain nonchalant. "It couldn't have just walked out of the closet. I'm sure it will show up, eventually." She never brought it up again.

Nothing filled that insatiable cauldron boiling inside of me. Not long after I stole the scarf, Ali came to visit me with her friend Sofia, who was wearing a fabulous pair of Chanel sunglasses. I'd never owned anything from Chanel before, either. In the blink of an eye, I swiped them right off the coffee table when

Sofia put them down.

The guilt was eating away at me. I couldn't wear any of this STUFF, so I kept it all tucked away in my closet. I ended up selling the scarf on eBay and hung onto the shame. Many years later, when I'd finally gotten sober, I was able to make amends. Tears threatening to spill, I bowed my head and told Maxie everything. Her reply made me even more emotional. She said that she'd known all along. "I overlooked things because I valued our friendship. I just knew that I couldn't trust you whenever you were drinking."

Things started spinning faster and faster, out of control. I'd disappear from work for days on end, hibernating in my apartment. After another argument with Wiley, I made an anonymous call to the Florida Real Estate Commission, slurring some really horrible accusations against him. He found out and not only was I fired, but he and Sierra filed a restraining order against me. They had been my closest friends, and I was even their son's godmother. All of my office friends stopped speaking to me and my world came crashing down once again.

Lemonade

I began working for my friend Marcus, who left *Travertine Investments* to open up his own office, *Edwardian Realty*. Marcus would have made the perfect Calvin Klein billboard model for The Mega Screen overlooking Times Square. Yes, he was that beautiful.

It was a great office, and Marcus was honest and hardworking. He'd never have allowed any of his agents to do anything that wasn't legal or immoral, which was a striking contrast to where I'd come from.

That's where I met my friend, Chaka Kane. With his bright blue eyes and dazzling smile, his angelic face matched his perfectly sculpted body. When he wasn't doing mortgages in the office, he was modeling in South Beach under the name of CandyKane. It made sense. Between Marcus and Chaka, it was like a candy store there. I'm glad I had the good sense not to sleep with either of them because we may not have remained friends all these years. Their friendships mean a lot to me.

While working at *Edwardian Realty,* Maxie and Dunkin invited me down to Key West for the weekend. They hoped that a relaxing trip to the Keys would help slow down my tornado of destruction. I promised them I'd be sober for the trip. I lied.

I started drinking before I even got out of Miami, arriving with a bag full of mini vodka bottles hidden in my suitcase. I unpacked and hid them around my bedroom and the rest of the house. What I couldn't hide was the fact that I was still drinking.

I spent most of my time lying on a raft in the pool drinking vodka and lemonade, my drink of choice. Dunkin's brother Trevor, who I'd known for a while, was also visiting for the weekend. Trev and I had always hit it off, so it was no surprise that we started sleeping together. Maybe it was all the lemonade?

He grabbed my water bottle at breakfast one morning to swallow some aspirin and nearly choked in surprise as he gulped down a mouthful of vodka. It wasn't funny at the time, but today we actually laugh about it.

Dunkin had been having some issues with a few of his employees. He needed help at *Joe and the Beanstalk*, so I offered, postponing my return to work. I didn't bother calling Marcus, something he'd become used to by now.

Maxie and I became overnight baristas at *Joe and the Beanstalk*. I had no clue what I was doing when it came down to making the coffee, but I was very good at licking the crumbs and icing off the platters where the cookies and cakes were displayed. Truth be told, I turned out to be more of a problem than an asset, so my career in the food biz was very short-lived.

I stopped at the drive-thru liquor store in Key West to stock up on vodka for the ride back to Miami.

Somehow, I made it back without getting stopped by the police. Or killing myself. Or someone else. Not the first time, nor would it be the last, that I drove HIGHLY intoxicated and managed to arrive safely to my destination.

LUV, BONNIE

Purple Rain

Let's be real. No one enjoys seeing their loved ones suffer. Especially when you idolize them. After years of neglecting his health, I watched powerlessly as my father's health plummeted from heart disease and diabetes. I watched as he puffed and gasped as he plodded from one room to the next. When he sank down on his comfy chair and watched TV, he would stomp his feet and flex his fingers back and forth to take away the persistent numbness.

He underwent a triple bypass, but returning to his diet of cookies, cakes and greasy fried foods only hindered the recovery process. The last time he went into the hospital, the doctors lost and revived him on the table three different times. It broke my heart watching him suffer for six grueling weeks in ICU. Intubated and laying propped up in the bed, he sputtered out the words, "I died." Tears welled up in my eyes. "I know.... not once, but three times. Did you see Grandma or Grandpa?" He nodded. I knew it was his time. His Angels were coming to get him.

It was a dreadful summer, driving back and forth from Miami to Delray Beach as endless buckets of rain pounded down on the roof of my car. It was a struggle to keep my eyes open after those long days at the hospital. I'd make two stops, first to the liquor store for some mini bottles and then to *Scoops*, for a large cup of ice cream. With skilled precision, I poured the vodka over the ice cream as I held my breath, hoping nothing would drip onto my lap.

I savored the first spoonful of sweet liquid as it slid down my throat and took off in my car, drinking and driving as I boomeranged the empty bottles out the window. I wonder just how many empty bottles, candy wrappers and empty bags of chips I've thrown out car windows over the years? Or bags of trash filled with junk food I wolfed down while driving or hiding in a corner of some random parking lot.

I gallivanted around the hospital with one of my father's Purple Hearts pinned onto the hip of my ripped designer jeans. My hips swayed through the hallways as I imagined myself walking down a catwalk in a fashion show. I was as thin as a rail and don't think it didn't cross my mind that I may meet a nice, good-looking doctor. My heart was perpetually racing from anxiety as I scarcely held on, just waiting for him to be free from his body that was sluggishly breaking down.

Perhaps the biggest ghastly moment during that time was when my father's plastic surgeon pulled me into the exam room and assiduously pulled open my father's chest with his gloved hands to reveal my father's beating heart. Eyes wide with disbelief, I stared down and winced. With no mask on and his face only inches from mine, I could feel his warm breath on my face. "We couldn't even save him again if we wanted to. There's nothing left here." Shards of glass ripped through my heart.

But my father didn't want to give up. It's frustrating but these things are never in OUR time... We don't dictate when it happens. I told him how much I loved him, that it was OK to let go and how grateful I was for everything he ever did for me. It wasn't until the night my mother (after me begging her to do so for weeks) at long last told him it was OK to let go that he passed into the tranquility of the night. He was a voracious fighter and hero until the very end.

No One Is Alone

The next morning, I received the call. "Bonnie? Your father died last night. Can you come up to the house and help me?" What the fuck was happening? I couldn't deal with my mother on a normal day, but of all mornings, this had to be the worst.

I had no clue where my car was. Oh, right. I was at Carter's last night. What happened again? Why don't I have my car? Why did I hitch a ride with a trucker on Biscayne Boulevard, barefoot, to get back to my building? Did I even have my keys or did I lose them? Where's my other Chanel sandal? With no car, how am I supposed to get to my car, wherever that is? If it's outside of Carter's building, there's no way he's going to let me back in through the security gate.

My head is pounding like nobody's business. I'm downright nauseous. How am I going to do this? And my father, I can't even think about that now. I wish my hands would stop shaking so much. I remember running and screaming in the parking lot at Carter's building, "That guy in apartment 4G has a dog. You don't allow dogs here, right?" What could he have done to incite such vengeance and craziness in me? What was in that brown paper bag I hid somewhere in his stairwell? His wallet? My keys? Did I take something from his car and hide it in the bag?

How I got to the car, whether I had my keys, it all remains a mystery. That sandal was somewhere between his place and mine, never to be seen on my foot again. How does someone lose a sandal? Or a car. Oh, yeah—all the Valium and alcohol unquestionably turned me into a monster. Dr. Jekyll and Ms. Hyde. Again. My head was spinning.

I arrived at what was now my mother's house. With no father to save me anymore from her. She somehow felt I was better equipped than her to handle all the phone calls and paperwork and arrangements that needed to be done after someone passes. The lonely only child, suffocating at the thought of me and her in that house without him. It was unbearable.

She beseeched me to stay with her for a few days, and I compliantly did as she asked. That night, I fell into bed in the guest room. I'd just drifted off when I felt a presence and my eyes shot open. Coco jumped up from my lap and was staring out the window. A little yelp escaped from her mouth. I'd purposely left the blinds open. There were no lights on outside, but we both gaped at this beam of light coming in through the window. It was unequivocally a sign—my father was letting me know I wasn't alone.

Somehow scattering his ashes was something my mother couldn't handle doing either. She sent me back home to Miami, about a 40-minute drive, with Coco on my lap and my father sitting next to me. In a box, in a shopping bag on the passenger seat. Of course, I knew it wasn't REALLY him, that it was just what was left of his physical body, but that didn't make it any less disturbing.

I scattered his ashes in the ocean and freed what was left of him. The more time passed, the more signs he would show me. There's not a doubt in my mind that he is young again, he is happy, and he is free.

It's only the ones that are left behind after someone passes that suffer. The ones that pass live on all around us and all we have to do is ask for signs and they'll show up for us. Even when we're not looking, they are there, watching over us, loving us, guiding us, and protecting us from harm.

Catch Me If You Can

Without so much as a quick wave, my mother jetted off to New York to seek comfort in her friend Lizzie's arms at her daughter Charlotte's beach house in the Hamptons. I was too busy picking up the pieces of my broken heart to care about her or anything else as I swam through a hazy cloud of sugar, pills, and alcohol.

My cousins Sue and Sheree encouraged me to move back to New York and stay with them. Being close to my Aunt Carol would surely make me feel more connected to my father. That, plus a geographical change, I could think of nothing better.

Not ready to commit to a permanent move, I sublet my fully furnished apartment to a friend of mine at *Corsi d'Acqua*, who was recently released from prison for running drugs for one of Colombia's most notorious drug lords. Friends in high places, indeed. After packing a few bags, Coco and I headed to New York.

When I told my mother, who was still jet setting through the Hamptons with Lizzie and Charlotte, her reaction wasn't surprising. "You're abandoning me NOW?" She never liked my aunt and cousins to begin with and this struck a hard enough blow for her to cut me off financially and to stop speaking to me altogether. It was the best thing that could have happened.

After settling into Sheree and her husband Arthur's basement, my new home, Arthur sat down and got right to work. He set his sights on creating an online dating profile for me, which he thought would fix everything. "All you need is to find a good guy!" Yes, because that had always worked out so well. Then I met Christopher. I was star-struck when he told me who his sister and brother-in-law were.

Gia, his sister, had risen to fame, starring on a soap opera that I'd been watching for almost twenty years. "THAT is your sister? OMG, I KNOW HER HUSBAND, TOO!" Tyler's face had been plastered on the covers of magazines and countless TV shows and films for years. His mother was one of the world's most famous and respected singer/songwriter/activists of all time. If I marry him, I'll practically be famous, I fantasized.

I moved in with Christopher two weeks after our first date and we stayed together for nine years. He didn't work and snorted OxyContin all day. When he ran out of pills, he'd find another doctor and get some more. Back then, you could walk into a clinic and get a script as easily as you could buy a loaf of bread at the corner store. I even went for him a few times, being the good codependent that I was. He'd dictate explicit directions about what to tell the doctor regarding my hypothetical back injury. Was it a herniated disc? C4? D6? B52? Oh, no, that was the new wave band. Oops, sorry Doc. My boyfriend made me do it.

When he couldn't get Oxy, he'd settle for Adderall.

He was up for days on end, fidgeting and wearing down his computer, installing endless new programs or sleepwalking back and forth from the bed to the fridge for a week, unable to even have a conversation.

I kept myself busy decluttering his messy apartment, rearranging furniture and swigging down every drop of liquor I could find. His patterns upset me, but I was caught up in my own destructive behaviors, so I accepted them.

I was outraged when he canceled our first trip out to California to see his family, which I was so eager to be a part of. Hours before our flight would have taken off, he groggily rolled over in the bed. "I can't go. I'm out of pills until Saturday and without them I'm going to go into withdrawals." WAS HE KIDDING ME? Scout, his daughter, was supposed to meet us at JFK in three hours. What did he care? He called his ex-wife and mumbled some sad excuse why we couldn't meet his 10-year-old child at the airport, leaving her stranded and having to fly to LAX alone.

We argued a lot and at one point, I even moved out, renting a tiny basement apartment near him. I slept on a blow-up mattress there for about a month until succumbing to the fact that it would be easier to move back in with him. My cousins and my aunt never liked Christopher from the start. "He's a drug addict," they'd say. True, but I was just as bad as he was. They wanted nothing to do with him and when I continued to stay with him, they told me it was going to be them or him. I chose him.

Christopher's only source of income was his monthly

disability check. He didn't grow up having money thrown at him like I did, and had no intention of supporting my extravagant spending habits. He couldn't have afforded to, even if he'd wanted to. Let's not forget, I was a spoiled brat.

I sold some odds and ends on eBay, but most of my income came from cleaning people's houses and apartments. I imagined myself flushing my college diploma down the filthy toilets I was cleaning with my mother's reflection staring back at me, wretchedly sobbing into my cap and gown. My housekeeping career was simple. I polished the furniture and polished off whatever snacks and booze I could find. It was only on the rarest occasion that I would be asked to come back and clean.

Seesaw

Ah, the mysteries of the mind.

I'd been on antidepressants since the age of 20, having been diagnosed with everything from Severe Depression to Bipolar Disorder to Borderline Personality Disorder. Addiction topped it all. It's hard to tell what came first, the chicken or the egg, not that it matters. The point is, I'd never been stable. NEVER. I was like a yo-yo my entire life, on and off antidepressants and psych meds like they were candy, and none seemed to prove effective for any significant amount of time.

Sure, there had been some fabulous "UP" moments in my life, but they have always been followed by a downward spiral. Then a violent crash. I could only be 'normal' for so long until everything just felt like too much. My head screamed, *I JUST CAN'T. I can't do ANYTHING. EVERYTHING is too overwhelming.* Then I totally shut down. I'll admit, it's been challenging. An enigma, for sure.

Life is wonderful. I'm so happy, I'm so grateful, I feel great!!

I'm having so much fun. I have everything I want and need. I have no problems at all.

Why won't they stop calling? Why won't they leave

me alone?

I'm so busy. I better slow down. I need to slow down. I have so much to do!

Why is everything such a mess? Why must I have all these papers everywhere? Why am I obsessed with writing down and checking everything?

Why does everything get so overwhelming?

Why does this keep happening?

Why did it get so quiet in my head? Why can't I focus?

Why can't I buy new clothes? I'm too fat to leave the house.

Why can't I do anything? Why don't I care about anything?

Why is everyone else so happy? Why is everyone else so busy on social media?

I'm so sad. Why can't I have fun? Am I the only one not going anywhere?

I hate everyone.

Why aren't they calling? Why don't they like me? Why doesn't anyone care? Why wasn't I invited?

Do I matter? Does anyone love me?

They said they loved me, so why do I think everyone

hates me?

Why don't I feel good? Why can't anyone help me?

Why can't I consistently show up for life? Will this noise and confusion ever stop? Will all these thoughts ever slow down?

How many days has it been? I CAN'T REMEMBER.

I feel so much better—of course they care.

What was I thinking? Look at all these texts and phone calls.

I feel so special and loved.

The Angel of Light and the Angel of Darkness. All rolled into one.

When my father passed, I stopped taking all my meds, so it had been a while since I'd taken anything for my mood swings. I couldn't function and I was broke. Christopher wasn't able to help, and I ended up going on welfare.

After an explosive fight with Christopher over him sleeping too much and not paying enough attention to me, I called the police. I was irrational and alternating between fits of tears and outbursts of rage. I was taken to the psych ward at *Coney Island Hospital* in a full-blown manic episode where I somehow extended the limit on all of my credit cards. With one quick phone call from my hospital bed, I ordered a ridiculous amount of extravagantly expensive furniture and home decor from

Mackenzie-Childs, one of my all-time favorite stores.

About three weeks after I was released from the hospital, a parade of white gloved men marched into Christopher's apartment to deliver and unpack these whimsical over-the-top pieces. There were so many items that they all couldn't even fit into the tiny apartment and I had to pay to have half of it sent back, white glove service and all.

The best thing that came out of that manic episode was finding a great therapist and doctor in New York who finally got me onto a cocktail of meds that seemed to work. For a while, at least.

Wind Beneath My Wings

After picking up the phone and hearing my mother's voice on the other end, I needed to sit down. I listened, surprised to even hear from her, as she told me about her health issues. "I've been very sick. I have some hemorrhoids and it's very painful. The doctors aren't sure what's going on." Making light of things, I assured her in an upbeat voice that hemorrhoids were no big deal. With a shaky voice, she called me a selfish bitch and hung up.

Several weeks went by when Lizzie called me. "Mommy (ironically, she loved referring to her as mommy as in 'Mommy Dearest') has cancer. She's very upset with you. You didn't seem to even care," she said. Maybe if my mother had TOLD me she had Stage 4 colorectal cancer instead of hemorrhoids, I would have taken the news a bit more seriously.

The next call I received was from Winston, her financial advisor and health care surrogate. "Bonnie, you need to come down immediately. Your mother wants to change her will and leave everything to Priscilla. I've known your mother for a long time and if she were in her right state of mind, she'd never do this. There are several checks missing. Can you see what's going on?"

Priscilla was my mother's nurse, who she'd known

for two months. I picked up the phone and called my mother immediately, telling her I'd be flying down with Christopher. Her response was terse as she told me not to bother coming. She said she'd changed the locks and wouldn't let me in. To make matters worse, Hurricane Frances was edging towards South Florida.

When we arrived, I told my mother we weren't able to get a hotel and, to my surprise, she let us stay with her. I was shocked by how frail she'd become after enduring radiation, chemotherapy, and a colostomy. No longer able to take care of herself, she'd hired round-the-clock help. The cancer not only ravaged her body, but also her mind. My mother just sat in her wheelchair waving her wand in her new role as Fairy Godmother to Priscilla, her three children and five grandchildren.

I have to give credit to Priscilla for taking my mother to church, the last place she would have gone prior to her getting sick. Her life was ending, but something had changed within her. She finally seemed at peace. Priscilla was a saint as far as my mother was concerned. She had also been managing her day-to-day finances. Peering into her checkbook, I saw Winston had good cause to be concerned. It was a mess. In church one day, I overheard my mother asking Priscilla what had happened to the $25,000 check she'd given her the week before. My throat tightened, my eyes wide open in disbelief. That was one of the missing checks Winston was concerned about.

People talk about untrustworthy financial advisors, and I am forever grateful Winston has been so loyal to my family for so many years. I don't know what I would have done without his financial advice. Not to mention his friendship, understanding, and kindness.

One day I stumbled upon a roll of undeveloped film in my mother's camera. I was unhinged by what I saw when I had it developed. Perverted photos of my mother lying in bed naked, and close-up shots of her stoma (the opening on the abdomen where the colostomy bag gets attached). There were also photos of Priscilla seductively posing in a tight, revealing blouse. What the hell had been going on here before I arrived? I was furious. It was time for Priscilla to pack her bags and leave. It would be a cold day in hell before she ever stepped into that house again. My mother wasn't happy, but she no longer had the energy to argue. Hospice came to the house several times a week, providing much appreciated comfort and care.

In the end, I was relieved by my mother's apology. "I'm sorry that I wasn't nicer to you. You never deserved the way I treated you. You were always a good girl." She told me I was her hero, and that she had always been jealous of me and she told me Bette Midler's song, *Wind Beneath My Wings,* always made her think of me. My heart nearly stopped. After all those years of hating her. I bent down and hugged her feeble body. For the first time in my life, I wasn't afraid of her. I felt sorry for her.

I told her how sorry I was for not being nice to her. She touched the tip of my nose with her index finger, forgiving me.

And so we were blessed with the gift of closure.

Freddy My Love

Relief washed over me after Grace passed. I scurried around for a few weeks, selling the house and taking care of what I had to. Exhausted, I boarded a flight back to New York. With no family left, I tightened my grip on Christopher and his. We got engaged and pooled our funds. I reluctantly agreed to purchase a home in North Carolina where his other sister, Meredith, lived with her husband, Andrew, and their two children, Olivia and Jonah. Andrew, whose first wife had been tragically murdered by an infamous serial killer, also had two sons who lived only a few miles away.

We all started a foundation for children with behavioral disorders, in honor of Olivia, and that's when I learned what a gift special needs children are. I adored the whole family, and they embraced me with so much love. I cherished our time together at family gatherings and especially loved singing in the church choir with Meredith and Olivia.

The only one missing from the family was Freddy, Christopher's father, who we left behind in New York. He always reminded me of my father with his big Jewish nose, great sense of humor, and captivating stories. Bursting into song every time we got together, I'd transform myself into Marty from Grease, belting out *Freddy My Love* for all of Brooklyn to hear.

I stopped drinking a few times during the nine years that Christopher and I were together, but I was always hanging on by my fingernails. Christopher had no desire to stop using drugs, and I blamed him for my relapses. The truth is that if I had really wanted to stay sober, nothing and no one would have stopped me. We constantly argued, and I was miserable. I thought I'd be happier without him, but dreaded the thought of letting go of his family. It was time to let go.

We'd been recording our expenses on an Excel balance sheet for years while I was maxing out all our credit cards. With my extravagant taste, I was always in the red, not him. We need to renovate the kitchen. I want a custom-made sofa. I have to have these boots. I won't be happy unless I drive a Mercedes. We can charge it, you have great credit. I'll pay you back. Christopher always just shrugged his shoulders. "If you want it, fine. But I'm not paying for it."

In the end, I owed him $30,000 plus my share of the $20,000 we still owed on the house I never really wanted to purchase. $40,000. I thought, *What about all the clothes I bought you? And the $50,000 smile I paid for since your old one made me cringe? Doesn't that count for anything?* It didn't. Because a gift is a gift. Christopher sued me for $40,000 and my attorney told me it would never make it to court. I couldn't haul myself out of North Carolina fast enough.

The Ladies Who Lunch

My attorney suggested I stay close to North Carolina just in case. I'd burned too many bridges to return to Florida and despite it having less than zero appeal, I knew three people in Atlanta. "Come to Atlanta," pleaded Brooke, a friend from elementary school, who I hadn't seen since then. That nice guy from one dating site who seemed to like me. And the bad boy from another dating site who was playing hard to get, so I decided he was the perfect reason for me to get in my car with Lucy, my sweet Maltipoo, and head to Atlanta. Coco, my Maltese, was now chewing bones and getting belly rubs with the Angels.

Brooke breezed in to help me unpack the morning I arrived in Atlanta, bringing a bottle of wine as a housewarming gift. She didn't drink, so I ended up drinking the entire bottle, plus another one, while she did most of the unpacking. By three in the afternoon, I'd passed out.

I got together with Joshua, the nice guy from the dating site a few times and even met his family, but he was too nice for me. He needed to pull back the reins. "We're so happy Josh brought home such a nice girl. Maybe you two will get married. We can't wait to have grandchildren!" Who wanted that?

The bad boy, Morgan, never could seem to find the

time to fit me into his busy tennis schedule and was just so arrogant. "I have tennis. I'm working. I'm going out of town to see my brother." I pursued him relentlessly. The less he responded, the more I wanted him.

One night, swerving through the unfamiliar streets of a new city, I desperately searched for Morgan's building. God only knows how, but I somehow stumbled upon it. In a stupor, I checked my makeup, pushed up my boobs, and rolled out of the car. "I need to see Morgan. I can't recall his apartment number." The concierge eyed me. "Last name?" I felt indignant. "I'm not sure." He demanded that I leave, or he was going to call the police. At the first sound of the cops, my face flushed and my body stiffened. Morgan would have to wait. I was out of there.

Back in the car, imagining the terror of getting a DUI then getting locked up in jail with the key thrown away in Atlanta jolted me out of my fantasy. Things were bad. Not just bad, but frightful. My life was in complete and utter chaos.

The next morning, I opened my eyes with a pounding headache and a twitch of impending doom. Immediately picking up the phone, I dialed 411 and after a few more calls was speeding through the streets to the nearest 12-step clubhouse. Upon arrival, I was greeted by a man named Don, who smiled at me and embraced me with a hug. "Welcome home." The warm feeling of familiarity felt so good that I got goosebumps. These people had suffered just like me. I was no longer alone. Tears streamed down my face. I began going to meetings and making new friends. At last, I felt a glimmer of hope.

Besides that clubhouse, there was a popular 12-step lunchtime meeting in a private back room of a chic local restaurant named *Penelope's Place.* That's where I met a group of women who formed *The Ladies Who Lunch Group.* To be clear, this wasn't a 12-step meeting, but the idea was for us to talk about recovery. Unlike 12-step meetings, only a few 'elite' members were welcome. We met every Thursday, alternating between homes. One residence was more extravagant than the next and it became a competition in which I was swimming just to keep my head above water.

Avery, in her Buckhead mansion, turned up her nose as she opened up a box of cupcakes. "Gigi's is the only place I get my cupcakes. Where are THESE from?" Scarlett's biggest problem was whether to take the kids on vacation with her. "Bali isn't a place for kids. Unless we bring the au pair!" Rayne (which ironically means queen) was racking her brains trying to figure out where Britt got her Gucci bag. "I went to Neimans, Saks, AND Gucci and they were all sold out. Where did you find that?"

Isn't this what I had wanted? To be included in the popular pretty people group? Here I was, Leo the Lioness, walking into the lion's den. But, as they say, be careful what you wish for. Wasn't I there for RECOVERY? I ended up relapsing, calling my sponsor, and telling her she was white trash and the only reason she had nice things was because she was married to a rich doctor. All but one of them dropped me faster than last year's Gucci handbag.

Stranded without a sponsor, ostracized by the group, and drinking AGAIN, I crept back to the original clubhouse I'd found and huddled in the back corner of the room. The people there were kind, genuine, and selfless. They wanted more than anything to be of service to me and anyone else that needed help. They placed value on the inside stuff and not on the outside. That is where I needed to be.

Candle in the Wind

I'd been sailing in and out of meetings and still found it nearly impossible to stop drinking for over two weeks at most. Then I met Zoey at a women's meeting in the clubhouse. She was a sparkling ray of light. Not a day went by where she wasn't smashing it in sequins, rhinestones, feathers or fur. Jewelry, cowboy hats, and every accessory under the sun.

She dressed to kill every day and even more so for holidays. Zoey loved her holidays. She was a modern Marilyn Monroe, a shining star. Just as beautiful on the inside as on the outside.

She took me under her wing, and I cherished the time we spent together. We'd zip off after meetings in her neon green convertible Bug for lunch, going on a shopping spree in one of our favorite thrift stores, or planting ourselves at an outdoor table at Pinkberry for some great conversation and frozen yogurt. We were always on the move. She was loving, kind, and nurturing, and a tremendous source of support for me. She had a brilliant sense of humor. "Nobody wants to be that old woman drinking and flirting with young men in bars and falling off their stools!"

Zoey showed me how she'd stayed sober for 20 years (and as I write this, 30 years) by leading by example. Part of how she did it was by doing lots of service, in and out of the rooms. A nurse by profession, she loved helping people. She volunteered at The Red Cross, Hadassah, and Dress for Success, just to name a few. She's given her heart and her time to help hundreds of people in the program, like myself, to get and stay sober. We had a very special connection.

Zoey said that I always reminded her of her daughter, Joy, who wasn't in the program then. I met Joy when she came from Connecticut to celebrate her Mom's 80th birthday party, a huge extravaganza with a Marilyn Monroe drag queen that was thrown by Zoey's adoring son Aaron. Joy would later become like a sister to me. I was blessed to take her through the steps of the program when she realized that she was actually an alcoholic and addict.

Wig in a Box

The Pinnacle was the most affluent fitness club in Atlanta. Only the best for me and my extravagant taste. I was crazy about the classes and the instructors there. Especially the dance classes, which have always lifted my spirit.

I met Jason at an event there one evening when I felt his piercing eyes on me from across the room— we had instant chemistry. He raised his eyebrows a bit when I told him I didn't drink, but quickly shrugged it off. After a few dates, we went out for Japanese food. "I'll have a Saki, please." Jason looked confused at my choice. I told him I rarely drank because it gave me a headache, but assured him I'd be fine. I wasn't.

We were together for about six months and things ended up pretty disastrous whenever I drank. There was a lot of arguing but I stayed with him because he was a mega successful businessman. Even though I was drinking, I still went to meetings. The suggestion was made that I stop dating because of my past patterns with dating and relapsing, but I wasn't ready to take suggestions. I kept drinking.

Wandering around Jason's house one day while he was busy working on his computer, I strayed upstairs into his closet. A box on the top shelf screamed out to me from high above. Unable to ignore it, I climbed up on the stepladder and reached out to grab it. One last poke and then there were two loud bounces on the floor. The lid popped off as I gasped in surprise. A toupee! OMG.

My father had worn one when I was growing up, but I had no clue that Jason had been wearing one this whole time. "Bonnie, what are you doing up there?" He thumped up the stairs, and I threw the toupee back in its box. His face flushed as he caught me standing awkwardly on the ladder.

I didn't feel bad for snooping through his closet, but I felt bad for him. I promised never to tell anyone about the toupee, but after our next big fight, I broke my promise. He was furious and wouldn't even speak to me. Back then, I didn't even know the meaning of the word integrity.

Not long after the toupee incident, I finally accepted my friend Cassandra's invitation to go with her to Happy Hour on a Wednesday night. I knew her from dance class and she was engaged to Helio from *Helio's Mediterranean Grill,* an iconic Michelin Star restaurant.

Wednesday Happy Hour at Helio's was THE place to go for singles. Live music and dancing combined with mouth-watering dishes and a candlelight ambience. *I'll show him,* I thought. *There are plenty of other guys out there!* I swung the heavy wooden door open, scanned the room for Cassandra and greeted her with an air kiss and those famous last words, I won't stay long. I'm just having one drink.

The bartender threw a spectacular show for us,

expertly flipping bottles in the air. Only the prettiest, strongest cocktails were good enough for Cassandra and her friends—a spectacular liquid rainbow in frosted martini glasses. One drink led to two and in no time, I was falling on the dance floor. Cassandra rushed over and helped lift me up. "You should eat something, Bonnie." That was the last thing I wanted to do, but I agreed, which in retrospect was a mistake.

The room spun as I climbed up the stairs to the upstairs bar. I lost my balance, sat down, and started vomiting profusely. If only I had eaten chocolate chip mint ice cream, like Minnie Minkelstein had suggested! The last thing I remember was the maitre d' escorting me to my brand new car, easing me into the passenger seat, and driving me home.

This time was different. The only way to describe the way I felt the next morning was pitiful and incomprehensible demoralization. No more. *Maybe I can have just one. This time it will be different.* I knew that if I had just ONE drink—it was over. Maybe not today. Or tomorrow. Or next week. Maybe I could control it for a month or a few months. Inevitably, it would be the same thing.

I knew beyond a shadow of a doubt that I could never pick up another drink or it would be the death of me. And that's when I got serious about my recovery.

I found a sponsor who had what I now wanted, and that was PEACE. Not all the outside stuff. Victoria suggested I work the 12-steps of the program as honestly, thoroughly, and quickly as possible. I accepted her suggestions because my way clearly wasn't working. So I did the work. That was over eleven years ago and I haven't had a drink since. THAT was the first of many miracles to come.

Eventually, Christopher won the court case. I got a legal notice from a North Carolina Court informing me that if I didn't pay up, the Sheriff could show up at my door and confiscate everything I owned. I panicked. Christopher knew that I had limited income from a trust and had no liquid assets at all, except for the jewelry I'd inherited from my mother and grandmother. There was no way I wanted to sell that.

Christopher had never taken his eyes off my grandmother's wedding ring and I knew that's what he wanted. The thought of selling it devastated me because it was like a piece of her. As far back as I could remember, she had worn that beautiful ring. A sparkling six and a half carat pear-shaped diamond. I loved the ring because of all its glistening beauty, but I had loved her even more.

I hadn't had a drink in about two months and was finally working the steps of the program. Had I not stopped drinking, I never would have been able to accept what was happening.

I was seeing the person I became when I drank, and it wasn't pretty. All of my character defects were glaring at me. And one of the biggest was how materialistic I was. A belief in something greater than myself was new to me and I knew that was the ONLY answer to a better life for myself. I realized maybe, just maybe, Christopher needed that money more than I did. Maybe that power greater than myself was doing for me what I never could have done for myself. We always have choices and our behavior always has consequences.

Had I not chosen to be with Christopher, this never would have happened. Had I not felt the need to spend all that money that I didn't have, I wouldn't have owed him that money. Everything I gave him was a gift. That didn't entitle me to not pay him back. I was the only one to blame for having to sell that ring. I hated him for the longest time until I accepted that fact.

It was just a ring, a material possession. My grandmother would be in my heart forever. No one could ever take that away from me. I was sober. I hadn't been drinking, and I was experiencing miracles every day. No material possession could ever buy me that.

So I sold the ring, along with a lot of other pieces of jewelry. I still didn't have enough money to pay off the debt, but Christopher agreed to a payment plan. After paying him a lump sum from the initial sale of the jewelry, I agreed to make quarterly payments for the next two and a half years. I finished working the steps and with every payment—I included a note. *Thank you for your patience in receiving this money. I hope you're well.*

Finally, I learned the meaning of integrity.

LUV, BONNIE

A Whole New World

When I returned to Miami, it was after I'd worked the 12 steps and it seemed like everything had changed. I was living in a new and sober world. I reconnected with a few old friends and I stayed in close contact with my friends from Atlanta, who were sober. It was important, though, for me to make new friends here that were in recovery.

There was a clubhouse in an old building close to the railroad tracks. You'd never know there was a 12-step meeting room upstairs just from looking at the building from the outside. In fact, I couldn't even find it the first time I looked for it. When I finally arrived, it was about 30 minutes before the meeting. The only other person there was Robert, a red-cheeked cherub who was working behind the coffee bar. People in the program are welcoming, but I didn't know anyone there yet, so I was slightly apprehensive.

About fifteen minutes later, a glamorous, vivacious blonde woman breezed in, hair tumbling down below her waist. She was dolled up in designer jeans and a pair of the most fabulous cowboy boots I'd ever seen. With her Gucci handbag flung casually over her shoulder, a huge smile lit up her face and in her soft southern drawl, she sang out, "Hi, ya'll! How's everybody doin' today?"

Oh boy, really? No one is THIS nice, I thought. Everyone that walked in seemed to like her and she really was as sweet as apple pie. Dobie Gray was a real life Southern Belle! She dedicated endless hours to helping people in the program stay sober. Dobie knew the literature inside and out and even led a weekly literature study. She was and is one of the most sincere and kind-hearted people I know.

When I asked Dobie to be my sponsor, she immediately threw me into service work, which made me extremely uncomfortable at first, but in the long run helped keep me sober. "Bonnie will take that service position!" *ANOTHER ONE?* I thought, rolled my eyes, and did as she suggested. By now, I'd learned that by helping others and getting out of my head was the key to staying sober. How true it is that we can't keep what we have unless we give it away.

I found the speakers for the Wednesday afternoon meetings, which meant that I anxiously reached out to people that I didn't know and asked them to share their stories at the meetings. I continued showing up every day at 12:15 pm and people started getting to know me. Only four months sober when I moved back to Miami, I could barely remember my own name.

Sometimes I'd meet someone, ask them to tell their story the following week and not even remember who they were when I saw them again. "I'm your speaker. Didn't you ask me to speak this week?" No one ever seemed to mind. They were kind and forgiving because they, too, had been in a fog when they first got sober. No one was judging me here. How delightful that was.

Dobie suggested I attend the business meeting. "Bonnie will be our new secretary!" I knew nothing about business meetings and didn't know what a secretary was supposed to do there, but I showed up at the meetings, took notes, and got to know the people who were committed to keeping that group up and running. I learned what to do, kept coming back, and I stayed sober. One day at a time. I made that my home group, and I began making friends. I had been blessed with an incredible sponsor and support group of friends whose intention was to better themselves. It was a refreshing new way of life.

Dobie started a private gratitude group on Facebook for some women she sponsored and suggested we list three things every day that we were grateful for. When we think about the good things we have, we don't focus on what we don't have. I've remained in that group to this day. Despite the challenges I've faced over the years in sobriety and no matter how difficult things may seem, I've found that there are ALWAYS things to be grateful for. A roof over my head, food in the fridge, and the joyous fact that I'm not drinking or drugging.

I'd kept my real estate license active but had no inclination to go back to that. I'd sold lots of things on eBay and told Dobie about it one day after a meeting, telling her I'd love to sell anything she wanted to get rid of. She was pleased with the suggestion. "I have loads of things in the trunk. I was just about to drop them off at the thrift store. Why don't you walk downstairs with Cash and I and I'll show you what I have?"

I loved Cash, Dobie's adoring husband. He was one fine-looking stallion. All class and as smooth as a cashmere sweater. They were both in recovery, equally dedicated to helping others, and just as kind.

Theirs was a fairy-tale love affair. When Cash popped open the trunk of their vintage Mercedes, my eyes widened. Stuffed into 15 Lululemon bags were the most magnificent designer shoes, clothes and bags I'd ever seen. I was blinded by all the sparkles. "Take anything you want, sweetheart," she generously offered.

I ended up buying from her almost as much as I sold. Ten years later, Dobie is my most loyal and favorite customer. And, more importantly, cherished friend. Inside and out, nobody shines like Dobie Gray. Cash is playing golf and riding horses with the Angels now as he smiles down on us all.

My friend Brynn and her family were, once again, hugely supportive of me when I came back to Miami. We spent a lot of time at her parents' home on DiLido Island and it felt so good reconnecting with them. We'd sit in the backyard staring at the Miami skyline and it was like I was seeing everything through a new pair of glasses. EVERYTHING seemed more beautiful. It was a whole new world.

I spent my first sober birthday, Thanksgiving and Christmas, at Uncle Jon's beautiful home where I finally met his wife Isabella and Brynn's cousins Giselle and Tyson, whom I'd heard about forever but had never met. I brought Lucy along and she got to play with all of their dogs. They've been like family to me. I've learned that family isn't always about blood.

I've been blessed with friends that I love wholeheartedly and who love me back, unconditionally. Sobriety has given me that.

About three weeks after I returned to Miami, I joined *Kokoro,* a luxury fitness club. That's where I met my friend Eli. We met in a body sculpting class and somehow (I don't believe in coincidences) it came up that he was in recovery. He was about ten years sober and asked if I wanted to be a guardian at *Elsa's Cottage*, a detox and treatment center in Fort Lauderdale. I had no clue what a guardian was. "You'll be great! You just have to bring in a meeting once a month to the treatment center. I've been doing it for years." I wanted to know if that meant I'd be doing the meeting myself. "Yeah, but it's easy. All you need to do is read the literature and tell a little of your story. You'll be giving them hope. It's helped me stay sober all these years." I was all for staying sober. So I figured why not give it a shot?

Eli put me in touch with Jacqueline, who'd started the program many years prior. I called her. "Well, normally, the guardians need to have a year sober, but as long as you've worked the 12 steps and seem so eager to get involved, let's try it." Those words just may have saved my life.

I committed to being there one Monday afternoon per month. There were days I didn't want to get out of bed, but because of my promise to show up and knowing that the people there were counting on me to bring in their daily 12-step meeting, I dragged myself there. I was only a few months sober when I started the commitment. I'd been irresponsible my entire life and had suffered from depression for years, so there were still days when I just didn't feel like doing anything. But I did it anyway.

Most of the residents at *Elsa's Cottage* were court appointed by a judge to avoid jail time, homeless, or returning to get clean again after MANY attempts at trying. Yet they were always grateful to see me. ME! All it took to turn my day around was for one person to tell me I'd helped them, that I made a difference.

Just by showing up, my self-esteem grew. I was becoming useful and getting out of my own SELFISH head. I was a guardian there until the beginning of the pandemic, which meant that I could keep a commitment, other than my sobriety, for over nine years.

I Am Changing

I flew back to Atlanta to pick up my 1 year medallion at the clubhouse where I'd gotten sober. My sponsor Victoria, whom I'd originally worked the 12 steps with, was there to present it to me and to support me. I was astonished when a girl came up to me after the meeting to ask me to sponsor her.

Victoria suggested I say yes, although I was terrified to take someone through the steps. "You've already done them and you're staying sober. You know what to do. Now you can pass on what you've learned. If you have questions, I can remind you what to do. It's very simple. If she stays sober, great. If not, it's going to help you stay sober." I was getting better at taking suggestions and so I took this one.

Her name was Carlysle, and she wanted what I had. She wanted SOBRIETY. I shared my experiences with her and she could relate. I gave her hope, and she needed that. All I could do was to guide her through the suggested program of recovery. If it worked for me, my sponsor, and for so many others, it would work for her. All she had to do was be honest, open-minded and willing. One day at a time.

Working with Carlysle helped us both. There were days when I thought life was unbearable and the ringing of the phone would infuriate me. I don't want to talk to anyone. How am I going to help Carlysle when I can't even help myself? My inner voice harped, *Pick up the phone. Just PICK IT UP!* When I did, she always ended up saving ME. She'd say things like, "You kept me from using. You helped me so much. You turned my day around. I feel so much better after speaking with you."

Carlysle is an inspiration because she's passed on the miracle of her sobriety to other people and she's still sober today. That gives ME hope. Together, people from all around the world can heal and grow stronger. I can't do this alone. During my eleven years of sobriety, I have witnessed miracles as I've guided nine women through the steps. The rewards are indescribable.

I watched them go from being hopeless for years to happy. Then they pass on what they've learned to others who are still suffering. The addictions that imprisoned me for so many years became my biggest blessings. I NEVER would have imagined those experiences would have enabled me to help anyone. Then again, no one is more qualified to help another alcoholic or addict, to give hope and shed light on their darkness, than one who has suffered the same.

Touch The Sky

I know today just how very blessed I am. As my precious Luna sits on my lap, drifting off to sleep, my heart is bursting with love. The sun's sparkling reflection on the water outside my sliding glass doors uplifts me as I watch boats passing by. I'm captivated by Angels swaddled in fluffy white clouds as they float through the endless blue sky. I'm free to explore the sounds and beauty of nature. The bright moon and stars beckon to me every time I step into the fresh night air. I have faith and trust in something far greater than myself.

There's a roof over my head. I'm healthy, have food to eat, clean clothes, a car, and money to pay for what I need. I'm responsible and accountable for my actions and live a life of honesty and integrity. Friends and family love me and I'm able to love them back. It's not all about ME today.

Above all—I have my sobriety. Without that, I would have none of this. Because of my sobriety, I have been given the ability to make choices—and I am free.

Freedom. Not everyone I know is that lucky. My friend Joseph is in prison today because he was in a tragic accident when he was 27 years old where a pedestrian was hit and killed. All tests revealed there were no drugs or alcohol in Joseph's system but there was a bicyclist that veered onto the road that caused his vehicle to jump the curb causing the accident. *There, but for the Grace of God go I*, is something I tell myself every day. I can't count the number of times I drove home and woke up the next morning with no recollection of how I'd gotten there or where my car was. It was a miracle I didn't end up killing someone.

Jo is creative, brilliant, kind and a talented artist. I'm proud to call him my friend. He expresses his heart through his art and spreads light wherever he goes. Justice is being served as Jo gets through his sentence with perseverance, patience, self-discipline, trust in God, and the support of his family and friends.

He's in the best shape of his life. Physically, intellectually, and spiritually. He's doing strenuous workouts and reading a vast amount of newspapers and books. He's enrolled in various educational programs, teaching classes inside the prison, and working on several art projects. In his words, his hope is to be released as a better man than when he arrived. I know he already is.

Joseph is an inspiration. There's nothing I wouldn't do for him. I've learned that the smallest things we take for granted are prohibited in prison. No sending gifts in bubble wrap envelopes, no stuffed animals, no cute little stickers on cards, or ripped out pages from a child's coloring book because they may be considered tattoo art. You can't even receive a call on your cell phone from a prisoner unless you have a special account set up with a private company connected to the Correctional Institution. Permission for a visit could take up to a year. The list goes on.

Freedom. Again, it's a privilege denied to many. I don't take mine lightly.

Before serving his sentence, Jo designed a limited edition series of Nike sneakers. Every pair was unique, with words spray painted on them. I cherish mine, standing taller in them, knowing that my friend created them. Someone animatedly stopped me in the street the other day. "Excuse me! Are you wearing Knucci's sneakers?!" What were the odds? I beamed from ear to ear—it felt like he was standing right there with us.

I'm touched and honored that Joseph volunteered to contribute his artwork for this book. Knowing that a piece of his heart will be a part of this project makes it even more special and exciting for me, that this book won't only be about ME. God willing, he'll be back within months after this book is released. I could think of no better gift than for someone to see one of his drawings and order a piece of Knucci art.

Joseph has already done so much for the community and continues to do so even now. Every morning when I wake up, I put aside a dollar. As the dollars add up, his days left in prison decrease. When he gets home, he's going to donate the money to his favorite charity, one that helps children and families impacted by chronic illness or loss. My jar started with one dollar and now there's a few hundred dollars inside of it. One day at a time.

With less than a year left, I pray Jo comes home healthy and safe. Life's about learning the lessons we need to learn. The harder the lesson, the more we can learn. There's a saying, 'God gave you His highest mountain to show others it can be moved'. Only when we're the one moving the mountain, we're not thinking about how we're helping someone else. It HURTS to move a mountain, and those watching hurt, too.

As you are moving this mountain, you inspire me to wake up every day grateful for my freedom and for everything else that I have, including your friendship. Thank you, Joseph.

Monster

Even though I was sober, I was still a mess where men were concerned. I still wanted a guy to save me. What can he do for me? What can I get from him? My motives were always questionable. Until we learn our lessons, we'll just keep repeating the same mistakes.

I met Wesley on a dating site when I was less than a year sober. He was decent-looking, but what drew me in were his impressive celebrity connections. What a surprise. He was an entertainment and sports photographer for a local news channel. That was enough for me to want to sink my claws into him. As a bonus, he was a Getty photographer, making him part of a talented community of individuals who travel the world for photos, attending the top sporting and concert events. I envisioned us traveling around the world—him taking photos and me socializing backstage with the stars. In reality, we only went to one concert.

I broke up with him over dinner two weeks after he brought me to Palm Beach to meet his family. We were out for dinner when he began eyeing my plate. "You know, you have some strange eating habits." I shot him a deadly stare and lashed out, "How dare you talk about MY eating habits when you stuff your face like a pig? Your stomach is like a giant marshmallow. Look what's on YOUR plate, not mine." This gave me the perfect excuse to break up with him. I couldn't bear the thought of having sex with him, and I couldn't put it off much longer. I just didn't have to be so cruel about it.

Then there was Javier. We met online and had great sexual chemistry, but that was about it. He had no ambition, was struggling to pay his bills, and smoked weed all day. The smoking didn't bother me because weed had always made me paranoid, so the main issue was the money, or lack of it.

After spending the night, he lit up a bowl, looked straight into my eyes and asked, "Can you spot me a $20 for gas?" Was he kidding me? "You know, if you didn't smoke so much, maybe you'd have money to put gas in your car. Or have the drive to go out and do something more with your life than teaching a few Karate classes a week. I can't spend my time with a drug addict. I wasted my life long enough. You need to leave."

Not only was I vicious, it's NEVER my place to call someone else an addict. That's for them to decide. I chose to be with him, knowing full well who he was, then persecuted him for it. "No one has ever attacked me so viciously." Those words rang in my head for the longest time.

Matteo was also in the program and we couldn't keep our eyes or hands off one another. He told me right off the bat that he wasn't looking for a relationship. Again, not taking his needs or what he wanted into consideration at all, I did everything in my power to MAKE him want to be with me. I was obsessed with him and deluded myself into thinking that the great sex would change his mind. It doesn't work that way. Sure, there was no problem getting him into bed, but getting him to commit to a relationship was impossible. That didn't stop me from trying. It was like banging my head against a brick wall.

Then there was:

Jack, a fitness instructor at *Kokoro*, set my body on fire. Throughout his dance classes, I'd mirror him, bumping and grinding until buckets of sweat poured down my body. Inevitably, we'd end up in bed together, especially since he lived in my building. After a few out-of-class bedtime bachata sessions, I woke up to reality. He had a girlfriend and was 20 years younger than me.

I wanted MORE than just sex. At least I thought so. So it was time for Jack to hit the road and I never went back to another one of his classes. He married, his wife got pregnant, and I was even invited to the baby shower. I was hiding in the corner, eating a cupcake, when he came over to me, fingers caressing the small of my back. "I'd love to get together with you one day." The cupcake crumbled in my hand. No thanks, Jack. I think I'll pass on that.

Gianni was a doctor who I also knew from *Kokoro*. I pined over him and dreamed of a life with this brilliant doctor, all the places we would go, and all the things he would buy me. He may have had money, but he didn't want to spend it on me.

Adam was another jackpot I met online who proved to be all bells and whistles. His profile read,

'Attractive widower looking for a great girl to travel the world with. Loves fine dining and enjoying life'. My bags were packed after our first date. The only traveling we did was from my place, to dinner, and back to his place. Sex was OK until one night he emerged from the bathroom wearing a full facial mask and a black latex jumpsuit from the neck down to his skinny ankles. He crawled over to me on his hands and knees, in a room that was quickly becoming claustrophobic, and handed me a horsewhip, begging me to beat him with this thing that wouldn't have injured my 3-pound Yorkie, Luna. I grit my teeth and my travel plans to Tahiti and Bora Bora were swept away like a tsunami.

Then there was Blake. A boudoir photographer with an impressive body, sexy salt and pepper hair, and a boat. The sex was full throttle, but the boat was always in dry dock. The only boat I ever saw with him was the one in his bathtub next to the rubber duck. Did he even HAVE a boat? The one in the tub wasn't cutting it for me, so I set sail to find another captain.

I was seething with righteous indignation and behaving like a monster, with no regard for any of their feelings at all. I even did intensive EMDR therapy because I was becoming a monster. I was so desperate to fill that hole inside of me. Nothing ever worked. It wasn't a person or thing that I needed. I needed a spiritual solution, and I was going to find one.

Purpose

All too often I ask myself, *Am I making a difference in people's lives?*

The switch flipped off again, and I was falling through the cracks. *Does anyone know how BAD this gets?* I wondered. With trembling hands, I picked up my phone and hit RECORD VIDEO.

I was disheveled, my speech low, monotone and labored. I had difficulty concentrating, speaking, and even just moving. It hurt to smile. I hadn't showered or brushed my teeth for days and I was pleading with my friend, through my tears, to kill me.

"I can't really say why this happened again, but clearly I'm a mess." I went through a litany of everything I'd eaten, sniffing loudly. I could barely breathe, the congestion was so bad. "I can't leave the house. I look and feel gross. Look at all the holes in my T-shirt." I pointed to all the holes in my T-shirt as I sobbed and continued sniffing.

"What's going to happen tomorrow? I really don't want to wake up, but I know I will. Because I've been trudging along like this for over six months. I'm slipping. Something's not working right. It's got to be some sort of chemical thing and I just can't bear going through more med changes. So this is me... Severely depressed, no drugs. I want to die. I don't know how I would kill myself. I don't know how I will ever leave my apartment or see anybody. I feel like a disgrace, a humiliation, a piece of garbage. Really, really low. I'm so sad. Luna, Luna, hey, baby. Look who loves me no matter what. Poor Luna. You have to endure crazy mama. I love you." I puckered my lips and made smooching sounds in Luna's direction.

"I just don't have it in me anymore. To do anything. I'm done. Look at these wrinkles." I pulled at the skin on my neck and chin through my sniffling.

"Crepey skin. I'm just done. So let's come up with some sort of plan. Where you can kill me, with some sort of poison. We'll figure it out. A traceless poison 'cuz I don't want to live like this anymore. I can't take it anymore. I'm tired. And when I turn 60, which is just in a couple of months, I get that money. You need money and I need to not be tortured anymore by this mood thing. Will you help me? I'm serious, I'm really serious. I don't want to be like this anymore—I just don't want to. I think you cared a lot about me at one point. So if you ever did, will you do this for me? As long as I know Luna is going to be safe, that's all that matters. I've lived enough. I have."

I hit SEND and off it went to my best friend Angel. I also sent the video to my friend Brandi, who was no stranger to highs and lows. Her doll-faced brother Brandon, now soaring with the Angels and watching over us both, suffered with bipolar for years.

Not long after that, I landed up in the psych ward at *The University of Miami Hospital.* I was there for 12 days and had three rounds of ECT. Electroconvulsive Therapy is a medical treatment most commonly used in patients with severe major depression or bipolar disorder that have not responded to other treatments. It involves a brief electrical stimulation of the brain while the patient is under anesthesia.

The hospital visit left me incapacitated. I was scheduled for seven more rounds of ECT (scheduled for every other day) and I couldn't, nor was I permitted to, drive. Angel would leave his house at 3:30 am, pick me up, and have me at the hospital by 5:00 am. He'd wait for me during my treatments and then bring me home, missing work if he had to. My headaches and mental confusion became increasingly unbearable, and I was wandering around like a zombie. After four more zaps, I could no longer endure it and discontinued the treatments.

Terror flooded my body as I floated through my building lobby, feeling like I was having an out-of-body experience. I saw people that had worked there for years and didn't even know where I knew them from. *Who ARE these people? Where am I? Did I have a stroke? Will my mind ever come back? How did I end up in the garage?*

Unable to function, Angel and his mom, Bianca, suggested I stay with them. It was a welcome reprieve as I was surrounded by nothing but love. It was me and Luna, Bianca and her husband, Angel's two dogs (Princess Leia and Kylo Wren) and Bianca's two dogs (Athena and Tulip). As I blindly roamed around the house, it felt like I was walking on a foam cloud.

Bianca and Angel did everything they could to bring me back to life. Bianca cooked my favorite meals, and Angel even took me to Disney World. I have no recollection of it. How does anyone FORGET a 3-day Disney vacation? Oh, yes, I'd just had my brain fried seven times. I stayed with them for almost two weeks. Angel drove me to *Kokoro* for a dance class and I didn't remember being there, either. Nor did I know who some of my friends were that I'd been dancing with for years.

After a couple of days back home, confusion and fear engulfed, once again incapacitating me. My friend TJ, despite having her own medical issues that day, showed up at my apartment to drive me back to the hospital. She was doubled over in pain, her stomach gurgling. There were tiny beads of sweat on her pale face. She reassured me through her own pain, as she sat by my side for eight hours until I was finally admitted. That's what you call a friend.

I felt so ashamed that I had to go back to the hospital. I was there for another nine days and I couldn't understand it. All I could think was, *I'm 8 years sober so I SHOULD be OK.* But mental illness is a whole separate issue. I was afraid people were judging me, but the only one judging me was me. That I've gone through so many psychotic episodes and NOT picked up a drink or a drug is miraculous. I didn't FEEL like I was sober, but I was. There were countless times that I wanted to give up, but I didn't. Whatever faith I thought I'd lost, whatever disconnection I was feeling, I still had a tiny spark of hope inside of me.

I finally started snapping out of what seemed to be a never-ending nightmare shortly after meeting Valerie at a 12-step meeting. She was new to the program, and to my surprise, I gave her my phone number. I had no intention of sponsoring anyone. Although, when she called me, I sensed the same willingness in her to do anything it would take to get well that I had when I got sober.

Valerie was struggling not to drink, and I'd been where she was and understood how she felt. Although I didn't want to drink anymore, I was struggling, too. Anything I suggested, she did. She WANTED the gifts that the program was offering her. I could hardly string a comprehensible sentence together, but I could somehow read the literature with her. Together, we read line by line and began working the steps, the suggested program of recovery. As the words and the work healed her, they healed me, too. I could share what I had learned with her.

Things that had gotten buried in my foggy brain resurfaced. She called me every day on her way to work. She didn't seem to care that my mind was mush because I shared the message of recovery with her. We carried each other out of the darkness and this beautiful and bright ray of light helped me more than she will ever know. After four months, on Christmas morning as we sat together outside *Starbucks,* we finished working the steps and she's been sober ever since. Whatever we do in this life, we are ALWAYS making a difference in the lives of others.

Lucy in the Sky with Diamonds

10.51 years 126.16 months 3842 days 92,193 hours SOBER. That's what the app on my phone reads today. *If only my weight was the same number of months that I have been sober.* Who the hell thinks like that?

Yup. After all this time. IS THIS THE ONLY THING THAT'S EVER GOING TO MATTER? No, not every day. Not all the time. It happens though. I slip back into it. Is anyone normal, though? What IS normal? For sure, I don't know. I've never been there. Have you? Has anyone?

Last night, I thanked my Lucy for sending me Luna. It was five years ago to the day that she'd passed. My Lucy in the sky with diamonds. She was with me when I got sober. I cried as I tried to connect with her as I stared up into the night sky and looked down at the shimmering moonlit water down below. The view from my apartment is even more beautiful at night than it is during the day. My Angels are always watching over me. Lucy is there, I am certain of it.

I fell asleep singing Luna lullabies in a slow, high pitched crazy person's voice. *La la la la la. La la la laaaaa.* I was feeling so sick to my stomach and could barely breathe because of all the food I'd eaten. I felt like I was somewhere far, far away, but I was right there in my bed. If there was a pill I could have taken before I passed out that would have prevented my waking up this morning, I would have taken it. No treatment facility or mental hospital can help me at this point. I just need to ride it out. It will pass. It always does.

I woke up in the middle of the night to go to the bathroom, letting out a long groan as I trudged to the bathroom like the Loch Ness Monster. I had to make sure my legs were pretty far apart because I can't stand the feeling of my thighs rubbing together when I reach this weight. Without a doubt, I feel a lot larger than I am. Body dysmorphia always kicks in after a few days of bingeing. I get excessively bloated, mostly around my stomach.

So far I haven't started bingeing again. I showered and I feel a little better. One minute at a time, one day at a time—I will keep trying. The minutes turn into hours, into days, into months, into years. That's how I did it with the alcohol, and by the Grace of God, that's how I'll do it with the food.

Days later, Daisy, someone from one of my 12-step Zoom meetings I'd never met in person, texted to ask how I was doing. I was annoyed that I even had to text her back. How quickly my tune changed from no one cares to why is she bothering me?

I picked up the phone reluctantly and read, "I've really been struggling with my eating disorder. The obsessive thoughts and behaviors are making me so depressed." I wasn't the only one, it seemed. We texted back and forth and a few days later, I woke up to another text from her. First time in months I didn't act out! (with a pink heart emoji) I'm so grateful for your friendship!

I HELPED SOMEONE. Just days out of being in the depths of my own despair. She was so happy and grateful that I'd been there for her, and it took absolutely no effort on my part. All I did was send out a few texts—she was the one helping me! Imagine that.

The next day, she texted to see how my day was going. It was actually going well. After our exchange, I wanted to reach out and do something nice for someone. Even if it was something as easy as sending a text. Even a simple text could make a difference. I COULD MAKE A DIFFERENCE.

Just as I was about to reach out to someone, I received a call from Jasmine. I often judge people because everything looks so perfect on the outside. She's gorgeous, successful, and bubbling over with sunshine. But everyone has challenges, setbacks and hardships. We just don't always see them.

"Reaching out was never easy for me, but you inspired me to do that, Bonnie. All the times you've reached out when you needed help gave me permission to do the same. It always made me feel good that I could be there for you. You helped me more than you'll ever know." Jasmine was there for me in some of my darkest times and nothing made me happier than doing the same for her.

Someone once said that it's selfish not to ask for help when you need it because you're denying those close to you the ability to help you. Your friends who care about you want to be of help when they see you in pain. We're here to give love, help others, and inspire people. Not to be perfect. We're just here being human. As long as we're still breathing, there is ALWAYS hope for things to get better.

LUV, BONNIE

LUV, BONNIE

Colombia, Mi Encanto

Two weeks before the height of the Covid pandemic, I boarded a plane to Colombia with Bianca. When our plane took off, I didn't know how life-changing the experience would be. I'd never been there before and Bianca had only returned once since moving here to the United States with her family when she was 16. She was the perfect tour guide, personifying everything Colombia and its people value. Faith, family, religion, and spirituality. Connection, beauty, love, strength, and grace. Gratitude, education, creativity, patience, kindness, and more.

Angel wings embraced me at every turn, with religious statues and churches as far as the eye could see. The horror stories, "It's all crime and drugs. All tourists get robbed and killed," are just that, a bunch of stories. Sure, you need to be careful. But that's true everywhere you go. We traveled to Cali, Medellin and Bogota. Each city graced us with its own remarkable gifts and spiritual experiences.

Nothing beat the warmth of the welcoming people of Cali, Bianca's hometown. They're good down-to-earth people who will go the extra mile for you. With no airs or pretenses. They don't just hear you, they actually take the time to LISTEN. With thoughtful attention and consideration.

We strolled through the cobblestone streets exploring the simple neighborhood pleasures. At the same time we were pushing our way through the crowded main street of the city, we could look up and see a peaceful river running right next to us.

Gathered together on an outdoor patio, sharing *arepas* and *limonada de coco* with Bianca's family was priceless. With our arms flailing, we made our best attempts to communicate with each other in Spanglish, roaring with laughter as we broke the language barrier. It was a beautiful thing.

Medellin literally took my breath away. The majestic Antioquia waterfalls were spellbinding. As if floating through a dream, the gushing water muffled the voices and laughter of the children and families playing and climbing the giant rocks. High in the clouds, everything glistened all around us.

Then there was *Piedra del Peñol,* a massive granite stone rising over 650 feet out of the flat earth of Guatape, with one of the most breathtaking views in the world. Winding my way up the 78-storey zig-zag stairway pinballed through a crack in the rock, I had to stop to catch my breath more than a few times as I climbed the 740 steps into the sky. The views at every turn were astonishing. Breathless, I soaked in the splendor at the top of the monolith, then wondered, *How am I going to make it back down?* It seemed like it would be impossible, so I needed to come up with a plan.

The steps were numbered, so I broke them down into decades. For each set of 100, I would reminisce about a decade of my life. That meant for steps 1 to

100, I would think about my life until the age of ten. I began the descent.

It was like I'd died and was doing one of those life reviews you hear about. I relived my entire life from a whole new perspective. With each new decade, those I'd loved who had passed appeared before me. It was like a flock of Angels were guiding me down the steps. "That white silk string that you found on your way up was from me," my grandmother confirmed. "I'm always with you." I looked down at the string I'd tied on my wrist earlier and a shiver ran down my spine. "I'll always love and watch over you." I was fifteen years old.

"Tell Isabella, Giselle, and Tyson that we're watching over Jon. He's not ready yet, but when he is, we're going to be with him." I was in my 30s and Hunter and Topher wanted me to pass on their message as they stood before me, so close and so real. Happy and free, like everyone else who came to me.

As I descended the stairs and re-experienced the decades of my life, my eyes filled with tears and I was captivated. Spirit to spirit, they carried me down. By the time I reached my 50s, it hit me just how quickly life goes by. As my body was gently placed onto the solid ground, I dropped onto my knees and thanked the Angels, God, the Universe...for my precious life.

Divine silence washed over us as we entered the quaint town of Guatape. After being completely submerged underwater many years ago, the entire town had been rebuilt. We chanced upon a shop next to a church with some creative gift items.

"Quieres unas galletas? O café?" asked the woman inside as her all-black lab ran over to us, wagging his tail and gaping at us with his puppy dog eyes. It was a lovely store, and we had a wonderful time shopping and chatting with the woman.

It was just past nightfall when we stepped outside to leave and spotted the black lab who'd left shortly before we did. He stood perfectly still against the stark white background of the church as shadows and light danced around him, revealing a distinct, large, white furry cross on his chest. I shuddered. Why hadn't any of us seen that cross before when we were playing with him inside the store? EVERYTHING about this country screamed out that God was with us, watching over us, and protecting us.

In Bogota, we visited *Catedral de Zipaquira,* Colombia's most famous cathedral, carved into an abandoned salt mine 650 feet below the ground. There are magnificently carved Roman Catholic icons, *The Stations of the Cross*, and *Angels* throughout the stunning tunnels of the salt mine. There's a basilica dome, chandeliers and an enormous, floor-to-ceiling cross illuminated with purple lights. Everything's carved out of salt and illuminated in the colors of the rainbow. Words can't even begin to describe the beauty and magnetism of this architectural wonder.

Also in Bogota, we took the 'teleferico', a cable car, to *Monserrate*, an enormously high mountain over 10,000 feet high with a church and shrine built in the 17th century. The views were breathtaking and, when we reached the quiet stillness of the mountaintop, there was a pathway leading to the church with the most magnificent gardens overlooking all of Bogota. Along the path were sculptures depicting the *15 Stations of the Cross.* It was another sacred and enlightening experience.

We were in Colombia for two weeks and what started as light chatter escalated to an uproar. "You need to get home. Covid is getting worse. Everything's shutting down. There's no toilet paper. I can't find any hand sanitizer." Blissful in our arequipe bubble, we paid little attention. We figured, *Surely, it can't be THAT bad.*

Angel called us several times, warning us the airports were shutting down, and switched our return flights home. Back in Miami, waiting for our luggage, someone standing a few feet away from Bianca and I let out a small sneeze and then screamed, "I DON'T HAVE THE VIRUS!" Her words echoed, nearly shattering all the glass windows inside the airport. Bianca and I stared at one another with our eyes wide in disbelief. Welcome home, indeed.

You've Got a Friend in Me

I was shocked that there really was no toilet paper to be found. Neither were there paper towels, cleaning materials of any sort, paper goods, water, or much of anything. It was like there'd been an apocalypse—shelves were bare and people were nowhere to be found. No one was leaving their home unless they absolutely had to, and the roads were all but empty.

Since Bianca and I had traveled together, she was considered to be in my 'bubble' of people, so I was thrilled to spend some time away from my apartment at her home with Angel and the dogs. We made the best of an unpleasant situation. We actually had a great time, all things considered.

I didn't mind the isolation at first. Zoom opened up a whole new world for us all. I see it as one of the biggest blessings that resulted from the pandemic. There were no more in-person 12-step meetings, so I started zooming all around the world. It was revitalizing to make new friends and hear new speakers sharing their stories, some of whom I felt closer to than people I'd known for years. Different time zones meant you could connect with people at any time of day or night.

My friend Maddie, from *Vibeology*, was a medium and invited me to one of her online events that she was doing with her friend Michael, who lived in

Spain. I've always been drawn to the world of spirit. Angels, mediums, psychics, anything related to higher dimensions. There must have been 30 people there from all over the world, but Michael connected to me immediately, bringing me heartwarming and uplifting messages from THREE of my loved ones who had passed. Their personalities and messages came through crystal clear. I began attending his mediumship events, meditation groups, and workshops. He opened up a whole new world for me, which enabled me to grow spiritually, find inner peace, and meet some great new friends.

After several months, the isolation started bringing me down. I went from working out almost every day for eight years at *Kokoro,* which was now closed along with almost everything else, to working out online or going for walks around the neighborhood. Even the gym in my building was closed. Suddenly, there were masks and suspicious eyes everywhere. City ordinances and my condo board stated I couldn't even walk 20 feet down the hallway to throw away my trash without wearing a mask.

Taking Luna for a walk was like walking through a war zone. People would see you coming and dart across the street in case you were transmitting droplets through your mask. God Forbid you sneeze, cough or walk within six feet of anyone. Fear permeated the air. There were no more allies in this new world. Everyone was perceived to be an enemy. COVID-19, The Coronavirus, had taken over.

It started with a stabbing pain in my chest, a horrific cough and shortness of breath. I'd just gotten home from Colombia and didn't give it much thought. Four months later, I woke up with horrible vertigo and nausea. Then it was a headache, chills, shortness of breath, and more coughing. The symptoms came and went, but when they came, they were bad. Just as I would start feeling good again, some new symptom popped up.

WAS I MAKING THIS ALL UP? It seemed everyone had something. I spent a lot of time lying on the sofa and watching the news, which became more and more alarming every day. WEAR A MASK. DON'T WEAR A MASK. EVERYONE'S DYING. VIOLENCE IS ERUPTING EVERYWHERE. People were scared, angry, depressed, and hateful.

I had no health issues before the pandemic but after ten months—I had a 7-inch folder filled with medical reports and scans. A visit to the doctor for my cough was followed by three in-office tests, six imaging scans, and office visits to seven specialists, including a pancreatic oncology surgeon. Apparently, I was allergic to 16 different things, had osteonecrosis of the right hip, COPD, an aortic aneurysm, a cyst on my thyroid gland, and a pancreatic cyst.

When all was said and done, I was sure I was dying from pancreatic cancer. Depression made me hope it was true. None of it turned out to be anything significant. If the pandemic wasn't enough to send me over the edge, that was.

On Valentine's Day, Angel and Bianca picked me up and drove me to the ER because my coughing had gotten so bad that I could barely breathe. My oxygen levels were fine and several hours later, I returned home. They told me nothing was wrong. It seemed the more stressed I became, the worse the coughing got. I was about to go down the rabbit hole again.

Hesitant to call my psychiatrist, I didn't want her to prescribe another new medication because each one brought on a whole new slew of side effects. I dismissed the thought of trying a new type of non-invasive ECT therapy (since the last ECT treatments nearly destroyed me). Desperate, suicidal thoughts raced through my head again.

Deep down, I didn't think I would go through with any of those thoughts because there are never any guarantees with suicide. I could end up being disabled or worse off than I was. So I decided to just give up on life. I wanted to sit in my apartment, shut out the world, and in some vain attempt hope to die. A week after the emergency room visit, Angel showed up at my house and I agreed to let him bring me back to the hospital. Only this time it wasn't for the coughing. It was my mental health that was the problem.

I stayed there for six days. The doctor changed my meds and Angel and Bianca took care of Luna for me. When I was released, Angel picked me up and took me straight to their house. I was there for three days and when he and Bianca suggested I stay longer, I declined, not wanting to feel like a burden.

Nothing changed when I got back home and I went back to doing the same things I was doing before the hospital, which was lying on the sofa and watching TV. The new meds were making me sick, and it wasn't long before I wanted to disappear again.

However, the last place I ever wanted to go back to was another hospital. For what? To get locked inside at the mercy of some doctor who knows nothing about me? With patients who most likely would have more serious mental health issues than me? Get served junk food all day long, sending me further over the edge?

It didn't take long before I was posting cryptic and disturbing messages all over social media. Alice in Wonderland falling down the rabbit hole, photos of people hanging off high ledges and lying down on train tracks. That kind of stuff. In a private sober women's Facebook group, I posted a photo of Luna that would have melted Cruella de Vil's heart, with the words, 'If anyone wants to take care of Luna for a while please let me know. I'm not sure if I'm ever coming back from this. Text me only. I'm not answering my phone'.

Then I cut off communications with everyone. Lesson learned here—post nothing distressing on social media. And respond to people showing concern about your wellbeing. Because on March 17th, the same day I'd been arrested over 20 years ago for keying Mason's car, my concerned friend Ariel called the police who showed up at my door, took me back to the same frightfully cold hospital, and Baker Acted me.

Bianca had a hunch something was wrong, so she came to my apartment to check on me, and found Luna shaking under the bed. She took her home and called me the next morning to let me know Luna was safe, putting my mind at ease after a grueling, sleepless night.

I was there for five more days and went home to Bianca and Angel's, where I now had my own bedroom. Bit by bit, I healed again. I never imagined when I walked into Angel's dance class over ten years ago that he and his mother would not only become my closest and most cherished friends, but my family. Their love and loyalty have been immeasurable.

Dancing Queen

When I first moved back to Miami, I began making new friends at *Kokoro*, mostly people from my dance classes. Most of them shared my passion for dancing and performing, and some of them have become my closest friends.

Jagger, the first dance instructor I had there, was an absolute diva. There was a group of girls, clearly his favorites, who'd been taking classes with him there for years. I desperately tried to ingratiate myself into their circle, all the while comparing myself to them all. *She's prettier, she's a better dancer, she has a better body—he likes her better than me.* But I truly loved his classes and made it a point to never miss them.

I was about to head over to the gym one morning when I found out that Jagger had been fired. You would have thought my world had ended. How dare he do that? To ME? Apparently, he'd pranced in late to class one too many times for management to look the other way. About a week later, when I'd gotten over my devastation, I returned to the gym to try the new instructor who was scheduled to replace him. I'd already decided that I'd never love another dance class as much as his. How wrong I was.

The new instructor sauntered into class, his baseball cap deliberately slanted down, just enough to cover one eye. He walked straight over to the sound system and began fidgeting with the music, not glancing up once. At precisely 9:59, he pulled his shoulders back, tipped his hat ever so slightly up to reveal his huge brown eyes, and strutted back to the front of the class. Eyeing him up and down, I mentally assessed with utter disdain. *Why is he wearing that ridiculous monkey T-shirt with those awful brown sweat pants?*

Then came the speech. "Hi, my name is Angel. I was a musical theatre performer for 11 years…" *WHAT? Maybe he wasn't so bad after all,* I thought. Hmmmm. "I've performed on Broadway and all around the world." BROADWAY? Now, my ears perked up. I loved the whole musical theatre thing and the hat, but what was with the clothes? I also didn't like that he seemed so detached. Cold. Unemotional.

After the speech, he cranked up the music, and the warmup began. Then we danced to some great songs. Lots of musical theatre and artists like Beyonce, Jennifer Lopez, Fifth Harmony, Shakira and more. Ok, so the music was great but my guard was still up. Until *Barbie Girl* came on. Thirty seconds into the choreography, when Angel cakewalked across the room, I lost it. His walk would have put most runway models to shame. He was a STAR, and I was hooked! This wasn't your typical left, right, right, left dance class. This was over-the-top choreography created by a genius. Not only was I watching a performer who was an INCREDIBLE dancer, but I was PART of the performance!

Every class began with a Paula Abdul song and

Angel's "UP, DOWN, UP, DOWN," militaristic barking and then it was curtain up! It was showtime. I was a star for one glorious hour.

Sober for only six months, Angel and his classes became my newest addictions. I had my spot in class, front row and stage left to Angel. No one dared take my spot. His classes took off like wildfire and quickly became the most sought after classes at *Kokoro.* While some found it impressive that these were highly intensive workouts that burned more calories than a spin class, that never phased me. My childhood dreams of being a dancer and a performer were coming true because I never felt like I was dancing in a classroom. I was on a stage! I was living my passion.

Angel had this beautiful quality of bringing people together. He was like the Pied Piper, teaching his signature class *Vibeology* in all the *Kokoro* South Florida locations as we all followed him from club to club. Men and women loved it. We called ourselves *The Vibettes.* There were *The Starlets* in South Beach, *The Divas* in Brickell, *The Trinas* in Coral Gables, and *The Dancing Queens* in Aventura. I'm not sure how we missed the boat with *The Real Dancers of Miami*, but it would have made a great reality TV show.

Angel uplifted us and we felt sexy, strong, vibrant, and beautiful. He never stopped reminding us we were ALL skilled dancers, and he helped us overcome our obstacles and fears. He encouraged us to own our unique individuality. We felt special and protected as he embraced us and swept us up into his world of magic, where anything was possible. His demeanor screamed confidence and his classes empowered us. Inside and outside of the classroom.

His stories and speeches never stopped motivating us—they never got old, no matter how many times we heard them. There is one in particular that stands out for me: "Like I say in all my classes, you have three choices when you encounter an obstacle. Option #1 (pause). You turn away from the obstacle and go, "I'm not doing it." That is not a WRONG choice, that is A choice. Option #2 (pause). You get through it, you do it, and you feel pride in getting through that obstacle. Option #3 (pause). You figure out a way around it. So you have three choices." Stated simply but with great impact. Then he'd carry on with class.

Angel had been bullied as a child, so he was always mindful of making everyone feel included. Outside of class, there were brunches, dinners, parties, and endless celebrations. Without trying, he was always the center of attention wherever we went. Everyone scurried to sit next to Angel. Small gatherings of three or four turned into extravaganzas of 20. Suddenly, there was a new game in town. Team Vibeology. People wondered if it was a cult.

I was shaking in my boots the first time I was invited to brunch. Angel's husband was going to be there and I couldn't wait to meet him. I was just a few months sober and wondered what would happen when the champagne corks started popping and I sat there drinking nothing but water. On the way there, I called a friend in recovery in a panic. "What will I say? What will they think? What if they don't like me?" "Bonnie, just show up and be yourself. If they didn't like you, they wouldn't have invited you. Get to know them and see if you even like THEM." When I looked at it that way, it seemed so simple and I ended up having a great time.

Then there were the flash mobs. We did one or two a year. We practiced the choreography after our classes for a few weeks and on the day of the performance, the entire group of us would arrive early, pumped up to practice, get dressed, and put on our makeup.

The first one we did stopped traffic as we danced together in the middle of Ocean Drive, one of South Beach's busiest streets. Seeing the joy and surprise on people's faces all around as we broke into dance was priceless. As thrilling as performing outdoors for a group of people felt, it wasn't about me anymore. It was all about what I could give to everyone that was watching. That's what made those performances so special.

Then came the *First Annual Disney Vibeology Trip.* Angel had been going to Disney since he was a child and he wanted to share the magic with us. He was the perfect tour guide and all he wanted was for us all to have a great time. There were many more Disney trips to come, each with their own special moments that will be cherished for a lifetime. Angel opened his home up to us for Thanksgiving and Christmas and I began not only looking forward to the holidays, but started loving them. All of us loved to dance, to perform, and to feel a part of something special. Thanks to Angel, we all did.

We were a group of friends from six continents around the world who each brought our own dynamic personality to the dance floor. Australia/Oceania, Asia, South America, Europe, Africa and North America. From places as diverse as New Zealand, China, Switzerland, Spain, Colombia, and Brazil. Venezuela, Russia, Turkey, and Israel. Lebanon, Canada, Germany, Mexico and Belize. Team Vibeology.

There was our beautiful and savvy mother hen, Tiana. A mogul in the travel industry. She was the voice of calm and reason in the group. Smoldering Elle, our New Zealand Kiwi filled with positivity, kept us laughing all the time. We watched her go from the arms of thugs into the glass slipper of her very own Prince Charming.

Bold and brazen, Kylie had a dazzling smile that could knock you out. She was our jet-setting entrepreneur and creator of her own successful protein cookie dough empire.

Sweet, elegant Kiki, with her generous heart of gold, divided her time between Miami and Pittsburgh with her handsome husband Ricardo, decorating their homes and visiting her two beautiful children and precious new grandson. A philanthropist and lover of the arts, Kiki was always terribly missed whenever she left us.

Sparkling Savvy was our extraordinarily talented designer who created a company with her best friend and handsome husband, Sandro, an award-winning architect. She was a beautiful ray of sunshine, ever reminding us how important humility and gratitude are.

Our roaring blonde bombshell, Tiffany, was a former Playboy Bunny whose zest for life was contagious. We could always count on Tiff to add some extra sparkle to any event.

Esme, our stunning barre and dance aficionado and part-time ski-bunny, was either dancing with us or sipping wine on the snowy ski slopes of Colorado with one of her many adoring suitors.

Mitzi was our ageless warrior. An avid activist intent on making our world a better place to live in. Nothing could slow this mother and grandmother down—not even two hip replacements.

Spicy vixen Star danced straight off the beaches of Rio into South Beach. With her platinum blonde hair and bronze tanned skin, she took over the role of selfie queen when Elle moved to California. Once that happened, her sexy husband Marco had to retire as our Vibeology Team Photographer.

Our effervescent Madison was our shining scream queen and successful creator of *Mia Spa and Wellness,* a chain of luxury spas around the world. All she ever wanted to do was *Dance with Somebody* and she finally found her dance partner. Cooper was 'Chicago's Most Eligible Bachelor' until Madison swept him right off his feet.

Then there were The Stallions, our male performers. Maverick, our racy, brilliant marketing whiz. Tony, our sexy high-flying theatrical aerial instructor. Toby, our lovable pony who never stopped looking for sunshine despite whatever clouds may have been hanging over his head. Colton, our sensual stallion who, despite his uncertainty of the choreography, brought the house down every time with his unstoppable enthusiasm.

Austin, our sizzling two-stepping Texas cowboy. Rhys, our heartthrob anesthesiologist who was born to perform. Zane, our beefcake accountant who was anything but boring. Enzo, our provocative pediatric surgeon with jet-black eyes who was as lean and muscular as a panther. Our Gabriel was a teddy bear until you poked him. Then, Oh Lord, watch out and wait for it. Hell hath no fury like a poked Gabriel. When he wasn't rolling around on the dance floor, he was out dancing with gigolos.

We called our Disney-loving Angel *Papimouse* and some would say it all started with a mouse. But before *Papimouse*, there was *Mamimouse*. We first heard about Angel's mother Bianca when he told us the story of her blasting Celia Cruz singing *Carnival* and vacuuming his room early Saturday mornings, stirring our Prince out of a peaceful sleep. The day we finally met her, we understood why Angel was as special as he was. *Mamimouse* was a stunningly beautiful, brilliant and inspiring ray of light.

People came and people went. New instructors began teaching *Vibeology* in Miami as Angel traveled back and forth to New York to teach the class there. As time went on, divisions ensued. People moved away. Personalities and egos got in the way. Life went on. Many of us continue to take his classes and there are always new people joining us.

We all share a bond that can never be broken.

Once you've been touched by the magic, you'll never be the same again.

Do You Want to Build a Snowman?

My cherished friend, Alice, owned *Alice's Palace: Wonderland for Pets.* It was a slice of Heaven for those of us lucky enough to have brought our pets there. A place for grooming, day care, boarding and love.

I knew my Lucy and Luna were always safe, loved and happy there. True, nobody could give a cut like Alice, but it was so much more than that. Alice was a force to be reckoned with. You either loved her or hated her and she didn't care what anyone thought. Her priority was the dogs. She was very selective and protective of them once she took them in. As soon as they walked through her door, they became hers. She'd built up a large and loyal clientele over the years because of that. She was everyone's Aunt Alice.

You felt like you were home the second you walked through the door. It was a charming house with a white picket fence and looked like something out of a storybook. The dogs could stay indoors with her or go outside through the doggie door into the lush Zen Garden filled with trees, flowers, Buddha statues and fountains, and comfortable chairs. For boarding, there was a magical bedroom suite filled with princess beds, fluffy animal pillows and squeaky toys for everyone. Even I wanted to sleep there.

Every birthday and holiday was a festive celebration with beautiful decorations everywhere. Alice had costumes for every occasion and loved dressing up the dogs in them, posting photos and videos on social media and sending them to us on our cell phones. But nothing compared to Christmas, when the house was transformed into a winter wonderland with a kaleidoscope of lights and decorations outside and inside.

My heart fills with joy thinking about all the times we'd spend the entire day decorating, placing the life-sized Santas, nutcrackers, snowmen and Christmas decor throughout the house. I can still feel the cottony snow in my hands and smell the sweet scent of sugar cookies like it was yesterday. We put up sparkling lights and scattered snowflakes everywhere and not a spot was left inside or outside for another decoration as we brought the house to life with the spirit of Christmas.

"MATILDA! TIGER! PUMA! COCO!" Her voice was booming. Sometimes she'd groom up to 15 dogs in one day. She loved what she did. After a long day, she'd collapse into a cushy chair in the Zen Garden, and all the dogs would jump up on her, licking her face as her head tilted up to the sky. She'd wrinkle her nose, laughing that infectious laugh of hers. "Remind me to ask your mother what she's feeding you. Why is your breath so stinky?" There was no sugarcoating with Alice.

I trusted Alice's judgement on what food to buy, what treats to give and what vet to use. On Coco's last morning, after a night filled with terrifying seizures, I called Alice on her cell phone at 6:30 am for help.

The vet hadn't opened yet. "Bring her here," she said, without hesitation. She made me tea and toast and sat with me until I could get her to the vet. I'll never forget that.

After Coco passed and I got Luna, I took her to meet Alice. "Leave her with me for a few hours. She needs to learn how to socialize with other animals." Luna was five months old and only 1.5 pounds. She was terrified, but I trusted Alice implicitly. I left with confidence even though Luna was cowering in the corner. A few hours later, when I picked her up, she was running around, playing with the other dogs and didn't want to leave. "If you treat them like glass, they'll break. They're stronger than you think. They're dogs, not people. It's your responsibility to be a good parent. That means letting her play with other dogs." Alice was so much more than just my groomer. She was a dear friend.

I adored her. Like the tides, everything changes. Nothing stays the same. Alice recently lost her battle with lung cancer. People live on in spirit, and genuine connections can never be broken. Love never dies. Souls never forget. We may not speak to people, but if you love someone, that love will remain throughout time and space, even if they aren't physically near you. Alice will be with me always.

For the
First Time in Forever

The past ten months? Well, it's the rainbow after the storm.

A few days after I returned home, I went for a walk in the park with my friend Julia and we started talking about her book that was about to be launched. Later that week, my friend Michael told me about the book that he was writing. The following week I heard my friend Cupcake, a best-selling author, speak at a meeting. Her story riveted and inspired me. In only one month, three people that I knew had written, or were writing books. I thought, I've always loved to write. I CAN DO THAT.

I wondered if I should write everything by hand, but when I started typing on my laptop, it was hard to even keep up with what was pouring out of my head. Writing by hand would have been out of the question.

One snippet turned into another and then another. My friend Michael suggested I contact Leigh, his editor, who he highly recommended. So I contacted her, and she agreed to help me. She encouraged me to keep writing, so I did. There were more and more pieces, and I didn't see how any of them could ever flow together. *There's no order to this. How is anyone supposed to make sense of it all?* I wondered. "I'll help you, Bonnie. Don't worry about anything." So I didn't. We started putting the pieces together, like a jigsaw puzzle. My writing improved with each new suggestion she gave me. As the story began to flow, Leigh kept cheering me on.

There were days I wondered if I should even continue writing because I didn't know if my words would help anyone. *Would people judge me? Was my writing boring? Would I offend anyone?* I kept writing through the doubts. I sent my friends little bits to read, and they encouraged me to keep writing. So I wrote, and I wrote, and then I wrote some more.

I wondered what the point was and started questioning myself. *Why was I doing this? Did I have anything positive to say, or was everything just so dark?* My fear subsided as I kept pushing myself, encouraged by the realization that I was no longer that person. The more I revisited those dark places, the more I was able to see the person I had become—who I am today.

I finally understand that I don't need anyone to save me. It's my responsibility to take care of myself. I've been on and off the horse so many times and I'll keep getting back on if I need to. I'm on the other side of the rainbow now—I'm still here and there's a reason for that. Maybe it's OK not to be OK. Maybe all those roller coaster rides haven't been for nothing.

Reliving some of these stories has been cathartic, exhausting, wonderful and at times bone-crushingly painful. You don't just write the story. You write, then write and edit and re-edit so you're reliving some of these things over and over again. I had no idea just how deep the pain was. I've talked about these things before in therapy, to friends, and even written and discussed them in recovery as part of the healing process. Somehow, this was different. It was more intense than ever before.

This book, my story, is right here—sparkling and no one can ever take it away from me. The only thing better than that would be YOU, the reader, getting as much good out of it as I have.

I've been so passionate about this entire experience. For the first time in FOREVER, I'm not looking to anyone or anything for my happiness. This passion, this overwhelming joy and sense of fulfillment, is coming from inside of me, flowing from something far greater than myself. The same force that was carrying me through all the shattered storms of my life has never left my side. And never will.

LUV, BONNIE

Happily Ever After

The gifts of sobriety have allowed me to dive freely into life with my heart wide open. I'm not the same person I used to be because I now have the tools to face today and the future with strength, hope, confidence, honesty, faith, courage, humility and integrity. With LOVE for myself and others. I'm productive and responsible. I take none of this for granted and am grateful for it all.

I strive to grow spiritually and to pray for the willingness to connect and help others. For self-discipline, patience and perseverance. To be caring and kind and to find balance and peace.

I get to soak in all the beauty life has to offer and when I fall, pick myself back up. To experience new fun and exciting things to do and places to travel. To see the sunlight of the spirit reflecting all around me in the beauty of nature, the magic of creativity, and an outpouring of emotions that pushes me to feel alive.

It's the simple things in life that heal me today. Love, laughter, freedom, passion, movement, animals, music, singing, dancing, creating and playing. Soothed by the quiet stillness of prayer and meditation and by trusting in a power that's greater than myself. I don't even have to define what that power is—I only need to trust that it's there. I know I am loved so I don't NEED anyone to love me.

Through it all, I've learned that I have value and purpose. I have the power to make choices, which allow me to remain true to myself, so I no longer need to bow my head down in shame. I have everything that I need.

As WE look up and reach for the sky, there's no limit to where we can go. I didn't think I'd live past the age of 40. I was MISERABLE for so many years. My story came alive when I looked inside. But I couldn't do it alone. God knows I tried. All my struggles, my losses, and all my moments of splendor changed me. They made me who I am today.

There is ALWAYS hope, even when we don't see it. If you don't believe it, believe that I believe. You can reach out to me. We all have the courage to fly.

Luv,

Bonnie

I Believe

It's impossible to be honest with anyone unless I'm honest with myself. Being true to myself is my key to happiness. It will keep me living with integrity.

I must remain teachable.

I must always remain honest, open-minded and willing.

I must do the work to get the results I want. Making an honest effort, self discipline, perseverance and patience will help me reach my goals.

I must take responsibility for myself and my actions. Every action has a consequence.

No matter what I think someone did to me, it always comes back to what my part was in what happened.

I must admit when I am wrong. Promptly make amends. And be willing to make it right.

Resentments will destroy me. I must accept people, places and things exactly as they are. When something isn't to my liking, it is ME that needs to either change or accept the situation exactly the way it is or I will never be at peace.

My expectations will always lead me to disappointment.

I have all the answers within and all I need to do is get quiet and listen. There is something way greater than me, and that is where the answers can be found.

Selflessness wins over selfishness every time.

Getting out of self and touching another soul is everything.

We all must answer to our own concept of what is good, fair, and just. I must judge no one, and that includes myself. There is no right or wrong. Do no harm to others and treat others kindly and with respect.

There is always hope as long as we are still breathing.

I can place no one above me or below me. That includes friends, family and strangers. Unity, compassion, and brotherly love create harmony and peace.

My faith will get me through anything.

There is no light without darkness. They both will guide me where I need to be.

I always have choices. I choose to see the positive in every situation.

What others think of me is none of my business. By remaining humble, I stay out of self and can be of service to those around me.

Be grateful for everything I have and know that I have everything that I need.

Our friends are a reflection of ourselves.

Stay connected with others.

Taking a deep breath when overwhelmed and staring up into the sky will show me just how insignificant my problems are. It's not all about me. Constantly seek through prayer and meditation to do the right thing.

Give only from the heart.

Serenity and peace will inevitably bring me happiness and joy.

When I'm struggling with anything, the best thing I can do is to let it go. In letting go, it all gets done. There is always a solution. And the solution is a spiritual one.

If something doesn't feel right, it isn't. Always trust my heart.

Try my best to carry the message of love, hope and recovery into the world around me.

Forgiving others will set me free.

Loyalty is unconditional.

Think before speaking, calling, texting. And definitely before posting on social media. Pause when agitated.

Live my life one day at a time.

I can handle anything for just one day. Feelings will always pass.

Principles before personalities.

I may have done bad things, but that doesn't make me a bad person.

It takes courage to change.

Setting boundaries with self respect allows me to decide who and what is acceptable in my life.

Loss is inevitable, but we will never lose our precious memories. Our loved ones may leave, but they will always be with us.

Only by giving love will my heart be full.

Opening my heart to receiving love is a way of giving love. I must be willing to let love in as well.

Angels are everywhere.

Special Acknowledgements

Blanca Rojas Jones, for always opening up your heart and home to me. Your friendship is a blessing. You, **Miguel, Daisy** and **Venus** are so very loved.

Leigh Sanders, for doing such a phenomenal job of making this book come to life and for opening my eyes to the world of 'show, don't tell' writing!

Lucy in the Sky with Diamonds, for your Angelic light.

Grandma Rozzie, for your infinite love, guidance, and protection.

Mom and Dad, for all you've done for me here and from beyond, especially teaching me about love and forgiveness.

GSS, my soul mate. Although we are apart, we will always be together. I will love you always.

My first sponsor, for showing me THERE IS A SOLUTION always.

Sarah Coffee Burks, for your love, support and the immense knowledge you've passed on to me from one very special Blue Book.

Barbara Sammeth & Billy Sammeth, for understanding. Your loving presence and your signs both confirm the fact that I will never be alone in this.

Staci Kanter, for your patience and love as you walked me through the staircase with a new perspective.

Jacque Tanner Tarlton, for your daily harvesting, planting the avocado seeds and helping me to flourish.

Schatzi & Bubba Kassal, for including me in the St Luke's family and giving me the opportunity to be of service there.

Beth Abramson, for your friendship and encouragement for over 40 years. Your encouragement and support throughout this writing process has been endless, ever reminding me to dot my 'I's with crystals.

CC & **Dara Zinney**, for being like a mom, sister, and mirror into my soul.

Terri Finkelstein Lorang, for your special gentle and loving way of always leading me back to the solution.

Gregory Sanderson, for proving to me that Angels are real.

Michael James Ivers, for your loving guidance that expanded my heart to the world of meditation and spirit.

Beth Andron Eiglarsh, **Cupcake Brown**, **Michael James Ivers** and **Buck Winthrop**, for inspiring me to do this, leading by example. Buck Winthrop, your incredible way with words never ceases to amaze me.

To **Papimouse** and all of my fellow dancers for making me a part of the greatest ensemble I ever could have dreamed of!

Cynthia Rogoff Abrams, my **Kiki**, and **Angel Snoop**, for your generosity and unconditional love and support through the years, our spa days and our fruit salads!

Maria Vazquez, my Tia Maria, for always being the voice of love and reason and for all the laughter through the storms and hurricanes. There's nothing like a hurricane without a dog bag for Lizzie who doesn't like bones.

Melissa Blakemore, for your trust in me, which I value more than you know, your laughter and your positive, uplifting energy and outlook on life. No Gucci on the gravel.

Joseph Franco, for your courage, friendship and inspiration through the most challenging of times.

Helen Fajardo, for always providing a safe and loving home for Lucy and Luna. You are with us always.

Theo and **Lizzie**, for being the sweetest and most perfect Yorkie role models Luna ever could have asked for. We both love you so much.

Ruth Starr, for the time we spent together in your safe and loving home when I was growing up.

Arline, **Mona** and **Sheri**, for being back in my life. You all mean the world to me.

Dr. Mencia Gomez, for your medical expertise, guidance, and support. Your smile has helped brighten some of my darkest days.

To **all my sponsees** over the years who have trusted me to guide you through the steps, thank you for that honor and gift. You have given me more than you will ever know.

The 12 Steps I took that led me to a life I never could have imagined… for all that came before me… for all who walk beside me… and for all who have lost their way, may you find your way back. For those that we have lost to this disease of addiction, may you soar with the Angels.

Lastly, to **my Angels** and that power that is so much greater than myself, thank you for helping me to create this book and for guiding me every step of the way with this and everything else that I do. Your presence is seen, heard, felt, and cherished. It is EVERYTHING.

Resources

There are many resources available for those who want to reach out for help. I'm not qualified to offer advice, nor is this a self-help book, but I am happy to share some resources that can also be found on the internet!

Al-Anon/Al-Ateen
al-anon.org

Alcoholics Anonymous
aa.org

Anorexics and Bulimics Anonymous (ABA)
https://aba12steps.org

Concussion Legacy Foundation
www.concussionfoundation.org

Mental Health Awareness and Suicide Prevention
https://www.rabbihammer.com/spreadjoy

Miami Mind
http://www.miamimindopen.com
email: info@miamimindopen.com
786-223-7624

NAMI
National Alliance on Mental Illness
1-800-950-NAMI (6264)
www.nami.org/help

Narcotics Anonymous
Na.org

Overeaters Anonymous
https://oa.org

Suicide Prevention Lifeline
1-800-273-TALK (8255)
suicidepreventionlifeline.org

YourMomCares
http://www.yourmomcares.org

About the Author

Bonnie Salkow grew up in New York and has lived in Miami most of her adult life. She shares her apartment with her cherished Teacup Yorkie, Luna.

She's beyond grateful for staying sober, one day at a time, since April 6, 2011.

Luv, Bonnie is her first book.

About the Artist

Knucci was born in New York, grew up in Miami and studied in Boston and Hong Kong. He has traveled extensively including Israel, Jordan, South Africa, Spain, France, Germany, Greece, Croatia, Italy, Holland, Poland, England, China, Macao, Thailand, Philippines, Brazil, Perú, Colombia, Argentina, Uruguay, Costa Rica, Nicaragua, Panama, Aruba, Jamaica, Dominican Republic, Bahamas, and throughout the U.S.

Knucci is currently incarcerated and collaborated on the artwork for this book through correspondences from prison. He is hoping to be released in August 2022.

www.Knucci.com
Insta@knucciknowsnothing

Knucci
Art Gallery

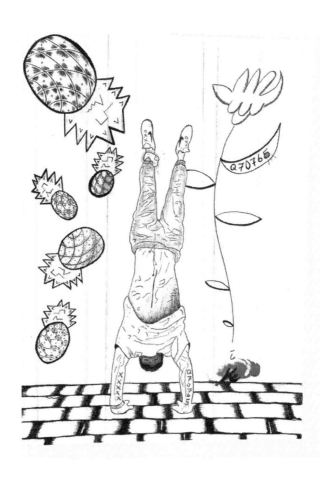

"3RD EYE INTUITION PINEAPPLE"
SIMPLIFIED + NO SHADING

2/27/22

FreeDumb™
Flower"

2/27/22

Q70765

Knucci

KN
'22

255

SIMPLE HEART
w/ ANGEL WINGS

2/28/22

Knucci
'22

KN
'22

257

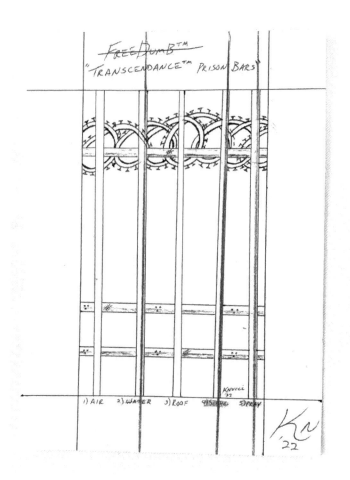

CRESCENT
MOON / DIAMOND

2/28/22

Knucci
22

KN
22

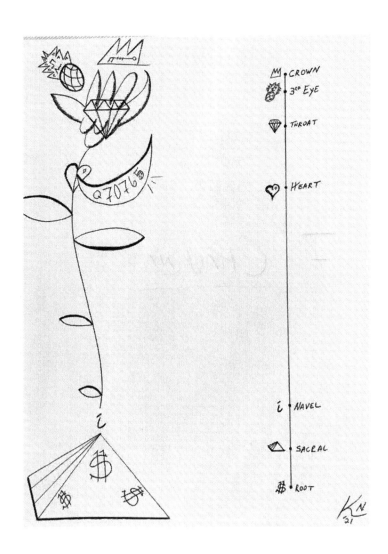

CROWN W/O KEY
+ CROWN W/ KEY

2/27/22

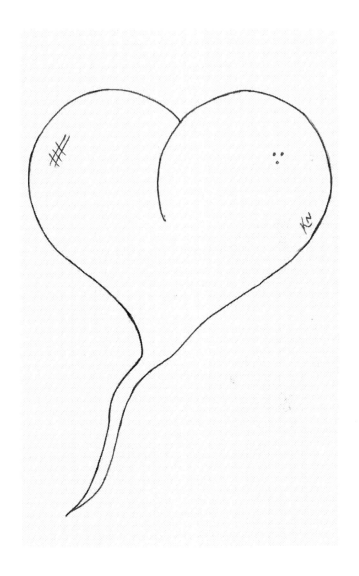

SIMPLE SHOOTING
STARS

2/26/22

Knucci

KN
'22

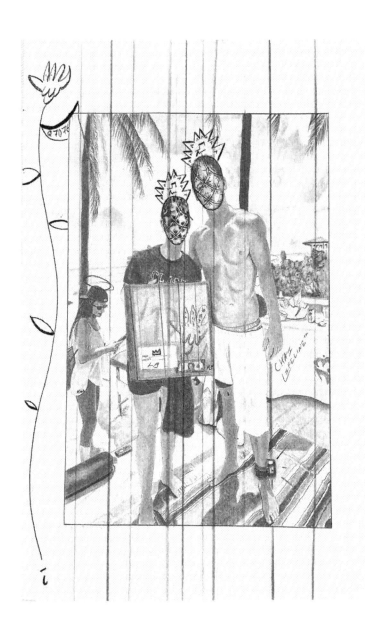

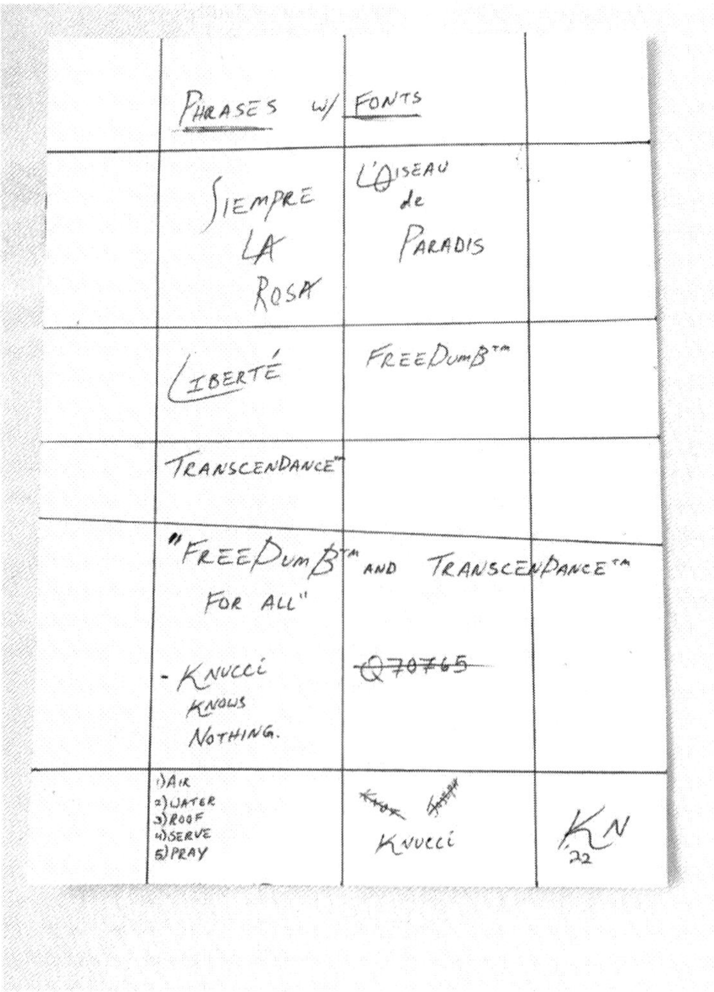
PHRASES w/ FONTS
SIEMPRE LA ROSA
L'OISEAU de PARADIS
LIBERTÉ
FREEDUMB™
TRANSCENDANCE™
"FREEDUMB™ AND TRANSCENDANCE™ FOR ALL"
- KNUCCI KNOWS NOTHING.
Q70765
1) AIR
2) WATER
3) ROOF
4) SERVE
5) PRAY
KNUCCI
KN '22

2/28/22

SIGNATURES

A)

K NUCCI

(B

KN

c)

KNUCCI
KNOWS
NOTHING.

KNUCCI
'22

KN
'22

267

Made in the USA
Columbia, SC
25 October 2022

70019986R00152